Carmela So... ...gin. Her family
is from Sout... ...ch are influenced by the
teachings of her mother and grandmother – but always with her own
... ...y of
... ...for
... ...ela's
... ...hat
... ...ned
... ...dio
... ...d a
... ...visit

Also available from Constable & Robinson

Soups for Every Season
How To Make Perfect Panini
Traditional Country Preserving
Afternoon Tea
Everyday Thai Cooking
Everyday Lebanese Cooking
Everyday Curries
The Healthy Slow Cooker Cookbook
Everyday Bread from Your Bread Machine

Southern Italian Family Cooking

Carmela Sophia Sereno

ROBINSON

To my patient husband James and my four children Rocco, Natalia, Santino and Chiara Boo, thank you for your support and believing in me. Love you all.

ROBINSON

First published in Great Britain in 2014 by Robinson

Text copyright © Carmela Sophia Sereno 2014
Illustrations © Firecatcher Creative, www.firecatcher.co.uk, 2014

The moral right of the author has been asserted.

A CIP catalogue record for this book
is available from the British Library.

ISBN: 978-0-7160-2374-6 (paperback)
ISBN: 978-0-7160-2375-3 (ebook)

Typeset by Basement Press, Glaisdale
Printed and bound in Great Britain by Clays Ltd, St Ives plc

Robinson
is an imprint of
Constable & Robinson Ltd
100 Victoria Embankment
London EC4Y 0DY

An Hachette UK Company
www.hachette.co.uk

www.constablerobinson.com

Contents

Introduction   vii

Antipasto   1

Stocks, Soups and Sauces   21

Bread and Pizza   43

Meat, Poultry and Game   67

Fish and Seafood   89

Vegetables, Sides and Salads   109

Pasta and Gnocchi   137

Risotto and Polenta   171

Biscotti, Cakes and Desserts   181

Italian Store Cupboard Essentials   209

Index   213

Introduction

Family and food have always been centre stage in my life. From when I was a child to my home today, food is exciting and very much a family affair. I married in my early twenties and my husband James and I have four beautiful children: Rocco, Natalia, Santino and Chiara. Just as the older generations of my family have taught and inspired me to cook, I have passed this love of food on to my own children. Natalia, my ten-year-old daughter, already loves to cook. She makes pasta for her school lunchbox and can rustle up some fresh handmade egg pasta with a simple tomato sauce. Unless you want your family to feast on take-away and ready meals when they leave home, engaging their interest when they are young is a great way to build their confidence in the kitchen and show them some basic skills.

It is sometimes easy to take for granted the lifestyle and opportunities we have today. Though my family had property, work was short and they were cash poor. Providing food was a struggle for many years, and at the age of five my father even had to scavenge for sparrows to have some meat in his diet. Tired of their impoverished struggles in the poor regions of Puglia and Molise and wanting a better life for their children, both sets of grandparents emigrated to Bedford, England, in the 1950s. Bedford was the chosen destination for thousands of Italian immigrants and still has a thriving Italian community today. Like many of their fellow countryfolk, my *nonne* (grandmothers) worked in the Meltis chocolate factory and my *nonni* (grandfathers) both worked at the local brickworks. They had a strong work ethic – starting with very little, but eventually buying their own homes. They used their knowledge of *cucina povera* techniques to shop wisely, cook simply and eat well. This is my inspiration. If my grandparents could feed their children on fresh seasonal food on the lowest of budgets, then so can we!

Cucina povera, simply put, means inexpensive fresh cooking. Using only seasonal ingredients when the flavours are at their best gives your recipe more zing and brings out the best taste. Fruit, vegetables, fish and game are always more reasonably priced when in season, which makes them perfect for today's busy, budget lifestyles. For those concerned with the environment, local fresh produce brings the added benefit of low air miles and supports your community. For Italians, if fresh tomatoes are not in season they are not eaten. Instead, plum and chopped tomatoes are preserved in the form of passata, which will then be used until the start of the next summer season. Whilst this ethos is shared, across the twenty regions in Italy you will get variation in how the ingredients are used. The more affluent north has a diet rich in meat and grains such as polenta and rice sourced from their paddy fields. In the south the warmer climate creates an abundance of fruit and vegetables which are paired with fish, shellfish and cheaper cuts of lamb and pork. Even the same dish will differ by region – a lasagne in Calabria will be different from one in Tuscany or Milan. From the top of the boot, down to the pointed toe, food throughout Italy is captivating in its variety with each region championing certain produce. Calabria is renowned for its *nduja* sausage, Puglia for its olive oil and Campania for its seafood and pizza.

For me, it was vital that I learn and recreate the much-loved meals from my childhood. With the help of my mother and *Nonna Carmela*, I have been able to achieve just that. It has been a great pleasure and a journey of discovery, on which I've learned about new ingredients and been able to preserve recipes before they are lost forever. I hope you enjoy making and eating these recipes – go on your own journey of discovery and don't be afraid to experiment with your own favourite, in-season ingredients. The recipes are simple and family-friendly, so please, join me in celebrating the pleasures of simple Southern Italian food.

Buon appetito!
Carmela x

Antipasto

I adore antipasti! The variety of dishes is endless and makes for a very indulgent time at the table. From a platter of finely sliced cured meats and regional cheeses, to bruschetta toppings, filled mushrooms, preserved pickles and vegetables and plump stuffed vine tomatoes ... it's hard to pick a favourite. Rustic bread is an essential accompaniment – together with time to enjoy the start of a wonderfully delicious meal.

Aubergine Parcels

Involtini di melanzane

A voluptuous looking vegetable with a beautiful, vibrant and eye-catching colour, the aubergine is loved and used widely throughout most family kitchens in Italy. These rolled and filled aubergine parcels are delicious morsels, perfect for part of an antipasti feast or as an accompaniment to a main dish of fish or meat.

Preparation time: 40 minutes
Cooking time: 20 minutes
Serves: 4

200ml olive oil
3 medium aubergines, sliced lengthways into 1cm slices
200g ricotta
1 egg
1 small shallot, finely sliced
50g parsley, chopped
¼ tsp grated nutmeg
Salt and pepper to season
500g simple tomato sauce (see page 38)

1. Preheat the oven to 190°C (gas 5) and heat 50ml of the olive oil in a large sauté pan.
2. Fry the aubergine slices until golden on each side. Do this in batches and allow to drain on kitchen towel to remove any excess oil. Add more oil as necessary as you cook: the aubergine will soak it up.
3. Put the ricotta, egg, shallot, half the parsley and the nutmeg in a mixing bowl. Season with salt and pepper and stir together well.
4. Lay the aubergine slices out on a clean work surface. Spoon 1 tbsp of the filling onto each slice, near one end, and roll the aubergine into a sausage.
5. Take an ovenproof dish and spoon in the tomato sauce. Lay the rolled aubergine parcels on top of the tomato sauce with the seam facing down and bake for 20 minutes.
6. Sprinkle over the remaining parsley to serve.

Bruschetta

Bruschetta

A fresh, crunchy, colourful vegetable topping tumbled over warm rustic bread is a mouth-watering accompaniment to grilled fish, baked chicken or a piece of flash-fried steak. The combination of vegetables can easily be changed to accommodate personal taste and to suit what is in season. Through the warm summer months, use tomatoes that have been handpicked and pulled gently from the vine along with fresh, pungent, homemade pesto. I make this topping and decant it into an airtight container or large jar; it will keep in the fridge for at least five days.

Preparation time: 15 minutes
Serves: 4

2 peppers, diced
1 red onion, sliced and chopped
1 small fennel bulb, diced
¼ cucumber, cubed
20 olives, pitted and quartered
1 large vine tomato, chopped
4 tbsp homemade pesto

1. Slice and chop the vegetables. Try to keep all the pieces roughly the same size. Approximately 1cm cubes are ideal, but rough and rustic chopping is fine too..
2. Mix all the ingredients in a bowl and stir well.
3. Put the bruschetta topping in a jar or cover the bowl and keep it in the fridge until needed.
4. Serve piled onto warm focaccia bread or alongside baked fish.

Eggs Filled with Tuna

Uova ripiene

A beautiful lightly flavoured recipe passed down to me by my cousin Ivana. Uova ripiene makes an ideal antipasti dish, accompanied by salad leaves and rustic bread. It is also a great store cupboard recipe and ideal as part of a picnic or midweek lunchbox filler.

Preparation time: 10 minutes
Cooking time: 10 minutes
Serves: 4–6

6 hardboiled eggs
6 anchovy fillets, chopped
160g tuna in brine, drained
25g capers, chopped
½ small lemon, juiced
Small bunch parsley, chopped
2 tbsp olive oil
Black pepper to season

1. Peel the hardboiled eggs and cut them in half lengthways.
2. Carefully remove the yolks, put them in a bowl and mash gently with a fork.
3. Add the anchovies, tuna, capers, lemon juice, parsley and olive oil to the egg yolks and season with a little pepper.
4. Stir well then spoon a little of the tuna filling into each egg white.
5. Place in the fridge until needed then serve immediately with a leafy salad or as part of an antipasti platter.

Fava Beans and Pecorino on Toasted Bread

Fave con pecorino

Generously slather this vibrant, soft green topping over hot, toasted sourdough bread for a delicious accompaniment to bruschetta. Prepare the topping by hand with a pestle and mortar, rather than in a food processor if you can, as this will add texture and keep the colour verdant and fresh.

Preparation time: 10 minutes
Cooking: 2 minutes (toasting bread)
Serves: 4

Salt, for seasoning
225g fresh fava beans
1 large clove garlic, sliced
10 mint leaves
30g pecorino, grated
Black pepper to season
3 tbsp extra virgin olive oil, plus extra for drizzling
1 tsp lemon juice
4–6 slices sourdough bread

1. Fill a small saucepan with water and add pinch of salt. Bring the water to a boil, add the fava beans and cook for 5 minutes.
2. Drain the beans and put them in a bowl of cold water. This will cool them rapidly to stop them from cooking further and will help the fava beans to retain their rich green colour.
3. Put the garlic and a pinch of salt into a mortar and pound it for a minute until you have a smooth paste.
4. Drain the fava beans and add them to the garlic with the mint. Continue to pound the mixture until you have reached a spreadable consistency.
5. Sprinkle in the pecorino cheese and season with pepper. Add the olive oil and lemon juice, stir and set aside.
6. Toast the bread and drizzle over a little olive oil, then spread over the fava bean topping and serve.

Green Anchovies

Acciughe al verde

Small anchovies (*acciughe*) are very well loved and are used in many sauces, salads and meat dishes. Similar to a full-bodied red wine, the longer the anchovies are left to mature in their tins the better, to allow time for the taste and flavour to develop. Every store cupboard should have a tin or two of these tiny, salty fish. Make this dish the day before you wish to eat it, as the flavours need time to develop.

Preparation time: 10 minutes
Serves: 4

10 anchovies, salted
2 tbsp white wine vinegar
1 garlic clove, finely sliced
Small bunch of parsley, finely chopped
½ small red chilli, chopped
4 tbsp olive oil

1. Wash the anchovies in a bowl of water to remove excess salt. Then drizzle them with the vinegar and rinse again. Pat dry using kitchen towel.
2. Remove any bones and skin and place the anchovies into a dish.
3. Add the garlic, parsley, chilli and olive oil. Stir well using a spoon, cover and leave in the fridge for at least 24 hours.
4. Serve on rustic buttered bread.

Mushrooms with Thyme

Fungi trifolati

Using a combination of different mushrooms helps to make this starter quite exceptional. A bowl of mushrooms with rustic bread as antipasto is my idea of heaven, however this dish could also go alongside some veal, lamb or fish. It's great fun to go foraging for mushrooms as long as you know what you are looking for! Whenever I think of fungi, Antonio Carluccio comes to mind. I wonder if that padrino of Italian food would take me foraging with my basket one autumn?

Preparation time: 10 minutes
Cooking time: 15 minutes
Serves: 4 (as a starter)

600g mixed mushrooms, sliced (portobello, chestnut, oyster, enoke, shiitake)
40g unsalted butter
4 tbsp olive oil
2 garlic cloves, sliced
1 tsbp fresh thyme leaves
3 tbsp parsley, chopped

1. Brush the mushrooms or clean them off with a damp piece of kitchen towel. Never wash mushrooms, as they absorb water very easily.
2. Put the butter and 2 tbsp olive oil in a frying pan large enough to take all the mushrooms. Add the sliced garlic. Gently fry the garlic for two minutes over a low heat.
3. Tip the mushrooms into the frying pan and stir with a wooden spoon. Sprinkle over the fresh thyme and 2 tbsp parsley, and cook for 15 minutes over a medium heat.
4. Once cooked, spoon the mushrooms into a large serving dish. Sprinkle over the reserved parsley and drizzle with a little olive oil, then serve with rustic bread.

Nonna's Figs with Gorgonzola and Parma Ham

Figs con gorgonzola e prosciutto di parma

Fresh, plump and voluptuous figs picked from their tree, still warm from the midday sun; are a Southern Italian delight. The fig season is so short that I like to enjoy them in their natural form while I can. However, Nonna's tree has produced an abundance of sweet, ripe fruit this year, so I thought that I would bake some just for a change, and they were absolutely delicious.

Preparation time: 10 minutes
Cooking time: 20 minutes
Serves: 4

8 plump fresh figs
200g gorgonzoloa
8 slices, Parma ham

1. Preheat the oven to 180°C (gas 4).
2. Take each fig, stand it on its base and, with a sharp knife, cut a cross half way through the top. Use your fingers to open out the fig.
3. Divide the gorgonzola into 8 roughly equal pieces and use it to fill the centre of each fig.
4. Wrap a piece of Parma ham around the body of each fig.
5. Place the prepared figs into a baking dish and bake until the figs have softened and the gorgonzola has melted.
6. Serve on a base of rocket drizzled with balsamic vinegar.

Pan Fried Courgettes

Zucchini fritte

Courgettes, or zucchini, are one vegetable that even novice gardeners can grow. It's good to have a variety of courgette dishes in your repertoire, to deal with the inevitable glut. I adore these fried zucchini, especially when they are warm in a sandwich.

Preparation time: 10 minutes
Cooking time: 20 minutes
Serves: 4

200g plain flour
1 tsp bicarbonate of soda
Pinch of salt and pepper
250ml cold water
Olive oil
2 medium courgettes, sliced lengthways, into 5mm slices
1 lemon, cut into wedges

1. To make the batter, mix together the flour, bicarbonate of soda, salt, pepper and water with a whisk. Place the batter in the fridge for 15 minutes.
2. Place a large frying pan onto a medium heat and add a glug of olive oil.
3. Remove the batter from the fridge and dip the courgette slices into the mixture to coat them.
4. Fry the courgettes in batches, cooking for 2 minutes on each side until lightly golden in colour.
5. Allow the slices to drain on kitchen towel to remove excess oil, then place on a plate and pop in a low oven to keep warm while you continue frying.
6. Serve with lemon wedges and salad.

Parmesan Soufflé

Sformatini di formaggio

A light and airy savoury dish to tantalise the taste buds. It's indulgent yet lightly spiced – and all in one mouthful. Bake these cheese soufflés in small ramekins, they will rise and have a wobbly middle.

Preparation time: 20 minutes
Cooking time: 35 minutes
Serves: 6

6 eggs
300g Parmesan, grated
100g pecorino, grated
250ml milk
250ml double cream
¼ tsp nutmeg, grated
Pepper to season

1. Preheat the oven to 180°C (gas 4) and grease six small ramekins with a little butter.
2. Put the eggs, Parmesan, pecorino, milk, cream, nutmeg and pepper in a large bowl or blender. Whisk well to combine all of the ingredients fully.
3. Divide the mixture equally into the ramekins.
4. Put the ramekins in a deep baking tray then add cold water so that it reaches half way up the ramekins. This will allow the soufflé to cook slowly.
5. Cook for 35 minutes until golden brown and set, but with a wobble.
6. Serve immediately.

Risotto Balls

Arancini con Mozzarella

With this delicious recipe leftover risotto need never go to waste again. In fact it's worth cooking extra so that you have enough to make arancini for the next day. Arancini are an absolute favourite with my children and family. They are delicious and soft with a hot gooey mozzarella surprise hidden within the crispy breadcrumb jacket on the outside.

Preparation time: 5 minutes
Cooking time: 6 minutes
Serves: 4

2 eggs
30g Parmesan
400g cold risotto
100g breadcrumbs
125g mozzarella
4 tbsp leftover tomato sugo (see page 38)
1 litre sunflower oil to fry

1. Beat one of the eggs and grate the Parmesan, then add both to the cold risotto and stir.
2. Beat the second egg and place in a bowl and put the breadcrumbs into another bowl, ready for rolling.
3. Take a small amount of risotto in the palm of your hand and flatten it.
4. Put a small piece of mozzarella in the centre, with a teaspoon of the tomato sauce, and roll the risotto into a ball.
5. Dip the risotto ball in the beaten egg, then roll it in the breadcrumbs.
6. Deep fry until golden brown.
7. Serve with a seasonal salad.

Aubergine Dip

Melanzzane caponata

In the height of summer when aubergines are in season they are velvety and deep in colour. They should be heavy, smooth and have an unblemished skin: handle them with care as they bruise easily. Softened aubergines are rich, yet mild and creamy, and taste beautiful spooned through pasta, or on the side of a meat- or fish-based dish. They are also perfect just with salad and bread.

Preparation time: 10 minutes
Cooking time: 40 minutes
Serves: 4

2 medium aubergines
1 onion
Olive oil
Salt
50g olives, pitted
220g sweet red peppers, drained amount from a jar
1 garlic clove
1 tbsp tomato purée
1 large bunch of basil, chopped
Salt and pepper to season

1. Preheat the oven to 190°C (gas 5).
2. Line a baking tray with foil, pierce the aubergines with a fork and place them on the tray. Peel and halve the onion and place on the tray with the aubergines. Drizzle over olive oil and a little salt and bake for 40 minutes.
3. Remove the aubergines and onions from the oven. Once they are cool enough to handle, peel the skin from the aubergines using your fingers and discard it.
4. Place the aubergine pulp, onion, olives, sweet peppers, garlic and tomato purée into a food processor . Blitz well for a minute and decant into a bowl.
5. Season with the salt and pepper and stir in the chopped basil.
6. Serve on crostini.

Softened Sicilian Aubergines
Caponata

Caponata is a combination of softened aubergines with tomatoes, onions and celery, dressed with a sweet and sour combination of flavours. It is traditionally from Sicily, but the recipe does vary through the region. It can be enjoyed as a starter, as part of antipasti or as a side dish to a main meal.

Preparation time: 50 minutes
Cooking time: 1 hour 30 minutes
Serves: 4–6

140 ml olive oil
4 medium aubergines, cut into 2cm cubes
1 red onion, finely sliced
1 garlic clove, sliced
60g sugar
390g passata
20ml white wine vinegar
2 celery stalks, chopped into small cubes and blanched in boiling water
Leaves from celery, chopped finely
60g capers, rinsed
140g olives, pitted, chopped
50g fresh breadcrumbs, toasted

1. Heat 4 tbsp olive oil in a frying pan, add the aubergines and cook slowly for 10 minutes until lightly coloured. Remove with a slotted spoon and drain on kitchen towel.
2. Add a little more oil and fry off the onion and garlic. Cook for five minutes then add 30g sugar, stir and caramelise for a further 5 minutes.
3. Heat the passata for 5 minutes and add the remaining sugar and vinegar and leave to cook over a medium heat.
4. Add the blanched celery to the onion mixture, stir and cook for 5 minutes.
5. Add the capers, olives and the onion mixture to the passata and stir.
6. Mix in the cooked aubergine and the fresh herbs then tip the caponata into a serving dish and scatter the toasted breadcrumbs over the top.

Stuffed Artichokes

Carciofi ripieni

Nutty in flavour and very beautiful in appearance, artichokes are used frequently in Italian cookery.

Preparation time: 20 minutes
Cooking time: 50 minutes
Serves: 6

6 medium artichokes
100g fresh breadcrumbs
40g parsley, chopped
50g Parmesan, grated
2 garlic cloves, crushed
Salt and pepper to taste
25ml olive oil, to drizzle

1. Trim off the top 2cm of each artichoke. Remove the tough outer leaves and cut off the stems so that the artichokes can sit upright.
2. Remove the choke of each artichoke (this is the hairy leaves in the centre) using a teaspoon.
3. Finely chop the stems of the artichokes and put them in a bowl along with the breadcrumbs, parsley, Parmesan, garlic, and salt and pepper. Mix well.
4. Pull the leaves of each artichoke open and fill the gaps with the breadcrumb mixture.
5. Sit the artichokes in the base of a saucepan and pour water into the pan so that it comes 5cm up around the artichokes.

6. Drizzle over a little olive oil and cover the pan with a closely fitting lid.
7. Cook until the artichokes are tender when pierced with a knife. This will take about 50 minutes, so check the water level from time to time to ensure the pan does not boil dry.
8. Serve in a bowl.

Carmela's tip

Into a large bowl of water add the juice of a large lemon. Place the artichokes into the bowl and this will prevent any discolouring.

Stuffed Portobello Mushrooms

Fungi riempire

There's nothing lovelier than a platter of large stuffed portobello mushrooms in the centre of a family dinner table, surrounded by antipasti pickles, salads and rustic breads. These portobello mushrooms can also be considered a meal on their own as they are quite meaty, earthy and woody. They are incredibly easy and quick to prepare and make a great starter to any meal, a delicious light lunch with salad or a side dish with meat or fish.

Preparation time: 10 minutes
Cooking time: 25–30 minutes
Serves: 4

6 large flat mushrooms, peeled and stalks removed
Extra virgin olive oil, to drizzle
Salt and pepper, to season
150g fresh breadcrumbs, homemade using slightly stale bread
2 cloves garlic, peeled and crushed
1 small red chilli, de-seeded and sliced (optional)
50g Parmesan, grated
1 tbsp oregano, freshly chopped
30g homemade basil pesto
125g ball of mozzarella, chopped

1. Preheat the oven to 190°C (gas 5).
2. Take each mushroom and cut out the inner stalk with a small knife. Peel the outer layer of the mushroom's skin with your fingers and place the mushroom in a baking dish.
3. Drizzle a little olive oil over the mushrooms and add salt and pepper to season.

4. Mix together the breadcrumbs, crushed garlic, chopped chilli, grated Parmesan, oregano and a little salt and pepper in a bowl.
5. Spread a tablespoon of pesto over the base of each mushroom.
6. Divide the breadcrumb mixture, spoon over the mushrooms and press down firmly, using your hands.
7. Sprinkle the chopped mozzarella on top of the mushrooms.
8. Drizzle over a little more olive oil and bake for 25–30 minutes until lightly golden.
9. Serve on top of a light leafy rocket salad.

Tomato and Mozzarella Salad

Insalata Caprese

Insalata Caprese is a very patriotic salad using colours from the Italian flag! It uses the simplest of ingredients – when tomatoes are in season, their flavour is so sweet they need little else. Any tomatoes are suitable to make this insalata, try using a variety for flavour and contrast, from a classic round to heritage varieties.

Preparation time: 10 minutes
Serves: 4–6

8 large vine tomatoes, sliced 1cm thick
Pinch of salt
500g fresh mozzarella, sliced 1cm thick
Pepper to season
Handful of basil, torn
1 tsp dried oregano
4 tbsp olive oil

1. Place the sliced tomatoes on a serving dish and sprinkle lightly with salt.
2. Drape the sliced mozzarella over the tomatoes, and season with a little pepper.
3. Scatter over the torn basil and sprinkle over the oregano. Drizzle with olive oil and serve immediately with rustic bread as a starter or alongside a main meal.

Tomatoes Filled with Tuna
Pomodori al tonno

The taste of sunshine in a single mouthful. Vine ripened tomatoes paired with tuna is a match made in heaven. Once the capers join the party your taste buds will explode. It's an inexpensive dish to prepare and can easily be made in advance.

Preparation time: 10 minutes
Serves: 4

4 large vine tomatoes
160g tin of tuna, in brine
50g capers, chopped
1 small onion, finely chopped
Small bunch of parsley, chopped
10 green olives, pitted and chopped
2 tbsp crème fraîche
Salt and pepper

1. Slice the top off the tomatoes, so that you can replace them like a hat.
2. Scoop out the inner pulp and seeds, and discard.
3. Mix together the drained tuna, chopped capers, finely chopped onion, parsley and olives in a bowl and stir.
4. Add the crème fraîche and season with salt and pepper to taste.
5. Spoon into the prepared tomato bodies, replace the tops and store in the fridge until required.
6. Serve on a bed of dressed rocket.

Carmela's tip
Capers may be small but they pack a punchy flavour and are used in many dishes through Italy, including in pasta dishes, chopped onto pizza and of course generously added to fish.

Homemade Ricotta

Ricotta fatta in casa

Making cheese at home always brings a smile to my face, partly because it evokes memories of living on the farm as a child. Mum would take great pleasure in making goats' cheese and sheep's cheese with fresh unpasteurised milk. I on the other hand make a quick and speedy ricotta which, simply spooned over crostini, makes for great antipasti or the best midnight fridge snack.

Preparation time: 10 minutes
Makes: 500g of ricotta

2 litres whole full fat milk
240ml double cream
1 tsp salt
3 tbsp white wine vinegar

1. Line the inside of a large colander with a double layer of damp muslin cheesecloth and place the colander over a deep bowl.
2. Pour the milk, cream and salt into a large saucepan and cook over a medium heat until the mixture reaches 85°C. Remove the pan from the heat.
3. Pour in the vinegar and stir. Curds will form after 2-3 minutes.
4. Using a slotted spoon lift the curds into the prepared muslin. Pour the remaining whey (the liquid) through the colander.
5. Allow the curds to drain for 30 minutes, removing and discarding the whey every 10 minutes. Gather the edges of the muslin and form a loose ball, gently squeezing out any remaining liquid. Allow to continue to drain in the fridge for a further 2 hours.
6. The ricotta can be eaten immediately, or it will keep in an airtight container in the fridge for up to 5 days.

Carmela's tip

Double the recipe to make filled cannelloni or beautiful ricotta and spinach ravioli.

Stocks, Soups and Sauces

Homemade stocks are an essential part of Italian cookery. They can be prepared in advance and frozen for up to three months. The carcass of a roasted chicken along with a few vegetables will make a flavourful chicken stock, or use up vegetables that are starting to look at bit sorry for themselves at the bottom of the fridge to make a vegetable stock. Nothing should go to waste. Use your stocks in risotto for a rich base and in fresh seasonal soups such as minestrone and *pasta e piseli*. Minestrone is one of our family favourites, with a mixture of small pasta and soft colourful vegetables, ladled with homemade stock and served with fresh rustic bread. A good stock base provides infinite options for soup – and Italians make soup with almost any ingredient.

Master a few basic sauces to begin with and as you build your confidence you can experiment more. A simple tomato sauce can be the base for so many different dishes or try a straightforward carbonara – silky, velvety and ready in minutes.

Pesto with Basil and Olives

Pesto alla Genovese

Pesto is incredibly versatile and great to have freshly available in the fridge. It takes no more than five minutes to make, and can be stirred through pasta, drizzled over a fresh punchy tomato and mozzarella salad or slathered over sliced rustic ciabatta. Its uses are simply endless. Pesto is traditionally made by hand using a pestle and mortar and lots of elbow grease. It is used up and down the country from region to region purely for speed and also has variations on flavour. Add a twist to a very traditional basil pesto: in this recipe I have added hearty green olives, very popular from the region of Puglia.

Preparation time: 5 minutes

50g pitted olives, green
50g Parmesan, grated
50g pine nuts
A large bunch of basil, 30 leaves
1 garlic clove, peeled
150ml olive oil and a little to store
Salt and pepper to season

1. Put the olives, Parmesan, pine nuts, basil leaves and garlic into a food processor and blitz. Alternatively use a mortar and pestle, in which case start by pounding the basil, then in stages add in the pine nuts, garlic, olives and Parmesan.
2. Slowly pour in the olive oil until you have reached a dropping consistency, season to taste with a little salt and pepper.

3. Spoon the pesto into a sterilised jar and then drizzle a little oil on top to cover. Seal and store in the fridge. This will keep for 7–10 days.

4. Serve with the bruschetta topping on page 3 or stirred through pasta.

Carmela's tip

You can substitute the basil and use spinach, rocket or a combination of both for variety.

White Sauce

Besciamella

The Italians have claimed this sauce as their own and so have the French. Although in my region we generally do not use besciamella, I felt that this recipe did need to be included in the book. Traditionally it's used over a lasagne or cannelloni dish. In Calabria besciamella is used to add a depth of flavour to baked pasta dishes.

Preparation time: 30 minutes
Cooking time: 5 minutes
Makes: Enough for a lasagne

130g salted butter
130g plain flour
1.2 litre milk
Salt and pepper to season

1. Sieve the flour to ensure there are no lumps.
2. Put the butter in a saucepan and place it over a medium heat to melt.
3. Whisk in the flour and slowly pour in the milk until the besciamella has thickened; this should take 2–3 minutes.
4. Season with salt and pepper.

Bread Soup with Cannellini Beans

Zuppa di fagioli

A warming soup using slightly stale bread, which helps to thicken the soup and adds a depth of texture. This soup is popular in Southern Italy – I found it being served whilst visiting Naples. If escarole is not available you could substitute the leaf with endive, kale or spinach.

Preparation time: 10 minutes
Cooking time: 1 hour
Serves: 4

500g escarole, trimmed
400g tin cannellini beans
2 garlic cloves, finely sliced
2 small sticks of celery including leafy tops, chopped
1 x 400g tin crushed tomatoes
2 tbsp basil, chopped
1 tbsp parsley, chopped
4 large slices bread

1. Blanch the escarole in a small saucepan with a little water for 3 minutes and then place the escarole into a colander to drain.
2. Take a large saucepan and fill it with 2 pints of water then tip in the cannellini beans and juice from the tin.
3. Add the garlic, celery and tomatoes. Season with salt and pepper.
4. On a medium heat cook and reduce for 40 minutes.
5. Add the drained escarole and chopped basil and parsley to the soup and stir. Cook for 10 minutes, check the seasoning and add salt or pepper if required.
6. Toast the bread and place one large slice or two small slices in the bottom of each serving bowl.
7. Ladle the soup over the bread to serve.

Bolognese Sauce

Bolognese sugo

A wonderfully simple tomato based sauce using minced meat. In Britain, this dish is consumed as part of a regular family meal with spaghetti, however in Italy, this would never be served with spaghetti, only with tagliatelle or papardelle. The sauce clings very well to the long thin pasta or makes a good base for pasta forno – baked pasta dishes. The sugo is cooked slowly and is superior to any other Italian sauce.

Preparation time: 15 minutes
Cooking time: 3 hours
Serves: 6

500g minced beef
500g minced pork
3 tbsp tomato purée
4 cloves of garlic, peeled and crushed
2 x 680g bottles of passata
350ml water
Salt and pepper to season
1 tsp dried oregano
Large handful of fresh basil, torn

1. Brown the mince in a dry saucepan over a medium heat, then drain off any excess fat.
2. Add the tomato purée and stir, then add the crushed garlic and mix. Cook for about 3 minutes and then add the two bottles of passata.
3. Mix well and slowly pour in the water. Then season well with salt, pepper and sprinkle in the dried oregano.
4. Simmer gently for 3 hours over a slow heat, lightly bubbling away.

5. After 2 hours of bubbling add half the fresh basil. I tear the basil with my fingers, so you have lots of uneven pieces, this will ensure the basil does not bruise.

6. When the sugo is ready it will have thickened and be incredibly tasty and deep with flavour. Then add in the remaining basil. Taste and check to see if more seasoning is required.

Tagliatelle Bolognese

Sugo Bolognese, served with tagliatelle, and lots of freshly grated Parmesan cheese is a crowd-pleasing favourite. Boil the tagliatelle for about 11 minutes (depending on the brand) till just al dente, still with a bite to the pasta. Drain, then return the tagliatelle to the pan and add 2 ladles of sugo to coat the pasta. Stir in freshly grated Parmesan – the more the better for lots of flavour. Ladle the tagliatelle into bowls and then add generous spoons of sugo Bolognese on top followed by more grated Parmesan.

Chicken Stock
Brodo di pollo

I like to make a large batch of chicken stock after a roast dinner. Roasted chickens work perfectly as they are already infused with fresh herbs and incredible flavour. I always roast two chickens instead of one, as leftovers are always a bonus. The carcass and bones are perfect to make stock for risottos and soups. Stock freezes very well too.

Preparation time: 15 minutes
Cooking time: 2 hours
Makes: 2 litres

2kg chicken carcass and bones
4 litres water
1 large onion, chopped
4 celery sticks, chopped
Celery leaves, chopped
3 carrots, peeled, chopped
Bunch parsley, chopped
Salt and pepper

1. Put the chicken carcasses along with any extra bones in a large saucepan and pour over the water.
2. Bring to a steady boil and add the onion, celery, celery leaves, carrots and parsley.
3. Skim off any foam and impurities that rise to the top of the water. Do this every 15 minutes, if required.
4. Cook for 2 hours over a medium heat, then season with salt and pepper.
5. Remove some of the larger bones and drain the stock through a strainer.

Carmela's tip
Store the stock in an airtight container, once cooled, in the fridge for 3 days or in the freezer for a month.

Fish Stock

Brodo de pesce

Lots of fresh fish is eaten in the south of Italy so stock can easily be made in preparation for a delicious fresh mussel and clam soup. When making stock, you must not use oily fish such as salmon, mullet or mackerel as it will produce a greasy stock. However, shellfish trimmings such as prawn heads and shells can be used. Fish stock is ready within 30 minutes and can also be frozen.

Preparation time: 10 minutes
Cooking time: 30 minutes
Makes: 2 litres

300g fish trimmings
1 white onion, sliced
1 fennel bulb, sliced
1 celery stick, sliced
2 carrots, sliced
Bunch of parsley, chopped
1 tsp peppercorns
2 litres water

1. Rinse the fish trimmings and put them in a saucepan, along with the onion, fennel, celery, carrots, parsley and peppercorns.
2. Pour in 2 litres of water and bring up to a medium heat..
3. Stir, then reduce the heat and simmer for 30 minutes.
4. As the 30 minutes approaches, remove any scum from the top of the pan.
5. Strain the stock through a sieve to remove the vegetables and fish bones.

Carmela's tip
Store in the fridge for 3 days or in the freezer for a month.

Green Sauce
Salsa verde

Traditionally, salsa verde is served with boiled meats known as bollito misto, however I like to serve it alongside fish and grilled meat. The sauce adds a sharp depth and can be changed and altered depending on your own palate. The best way to make salsa verde is to chop all the ingredients very finely by hand, which gives the best texture. However, for ease you can chop all the ingredients in a food processor and blitz to create a smooth sauce. Always remember to taste and check the sauce to see if it may need seasoning.

Preparation time: 5 minutes
Serves: 4

6 tbsp flat leaf parsley
2 tbsp capers, rinsed
6 anchovy fillets
1 garlic clove, crushed
1 tsp mustard
1 tbsp red wine vinegar
8 tbsp extra virgin olive oil
Salt and pepper to season

1. If using a food processor, add all the ingredients at once and blitz.
2. To chop by hand, finely chop the parsley, capers and anchovies and place in a bowl.
3. Add the crushed garlic along with the mustard and red wine vinegar.
4. Slowly pour in the extra virgin olive oil a little at a time, stirring as you pour, until you have reached the right consistency. This should be a loose sauce.
5. Adjust the balance of flavour with a little salt and pepper.

Carmela's tip:
Salsa verde will keep in the fridge for up to a week in an airtight container.

Lentil and White Onion Soup
Zuppa di lenticchie con cipolla

Having essentials in your larder enables you to make and prepare a quick light lunch or family dinner. The only added extra to this store cupboard soup would be some fresh bread to dip and to *fare la scarpetta*, to scrape the bowl of its sauces, a traditional Italian trait especially when sat around our family table.

Preparation time: 5 minutes
Cooking time: 30 minutes
Serves: 4

2 tbsp olive oil
25g butter
3 garlic cloves, peeled, crushed
2 large onions, sliced
1 large glass of white wine
1.5 litres vegetable stock
100g red lentils
Salt and pepper to season
1 small chilli, sliced
Fresh bunch of parsley, chopped
30g Parmesan, grated

1. Put the olive oil and butter in a saucepan, add 2 tbsp olive oil along with the butter then add the crushed garlic and sliced onion and soften for 5–7 minutes.
2. Pour in the white wine then simmer for a further 5 minutes.
3. Add the vegetable stock followed by the lentils. I use dried red lentils, which give a wonderful colour contrast.
4. Stir and season with salt and pepper and a chopped chilli for heat.
5. Simmer for 25 minutes until thickened. Taste and add more seasoning if required. Toss in a large handful of freshly chopped parsley and stir.
6. Serve in warm bowls with a little grated Parmesan.

Minestrone

Zuppa di minestrone

Using a basic soffritto (onion, celery and carrot base) adds immediate depth of flavour and texture to any soup or stew. This delicious minestrone soup is full of vegetables as well as the celery leafy tops; they are the best part of the celery and add an instant smack of flavour. You can use three fresh tomatoes in place of tinned if you prefer and use vegetable or chicken stock. Served piping hot on a cold winter's day, this soup is a hug in disguise.

Preparation time: 15 minutes
Cooking time: 45 minutes
Serves: 4

2 tbsp olive oil
20g butter
60g pancetta, cubed
1 small onion, finely sliced
170g carrots, finely diced
2 celery stalks, finely diced
Celery leafy tops, chopped finely
2 cloves garlic, crushed
200g tin crushed tomatoes
1.7 litres chicken or vegetable stock
1 tbsp tomato purée
Salt and pepper to season
Small bunch basil, roughly chopped
Small bunch parsley, roughly chopped
100g small pasta (short macaroni or ditalini)
40g Parmesan, grated

1. Put the olive oil and butter in a saucepan and fry off the pancetta on a medium heat for 2 minutes then add the onions and cook for a further 5 minutes.
2. Tumble in the carrots, celery, celery tops and garlic. Cook for 10 minutes then add the tomatoes and stir.

3. Slowly pour in the stock along with the tomato purée. Stir and season with salt, pepper and half the fresh herbs. Cook for a further 10 minutes.
4. Add the pasta to the soup and cook as per packet instructions.
5. Two minutes before serving stir in the remaining fresh herbs.
6. Serve in warm bowls with a generous grating of fresh Parmesan and rustic bread for dipping.

Meat Sauce

Sugo con carne

A traditional meat-based tomato sauce. It's so versatile that once you have mastered this simple recipe you can use it in endless simple *cucina povera* cooked meals. Slow cooking and simple Italian flavours, make for a welcoming centrepiece. Here I have chosen to use pork pre-cut ribs. An alternative could be polpettini (meatballs) or brasciole (rolled pork or beef). This sugo would be used to make and finish off a lasagne, cannelloni or parmigiana, or stirred through pasta and gnocchi.

Preparation time: 15 minutes
Cooking time: 3 hours
Serves: 6

6 tbsp olive oil
12 medium pork ribs, cut into individual ribs
3 bottles of passata, 680g per jar
400ml water
4 tbsp tomato purée
4 cloves of garlic, peeled, crushed
Salt and pepper to season
Large handful of fresh basil, torn
1 bay leaf
1 tsp dried oregano
1 small chilli, chopped

1. Place the prepared ribs in a large saucepan and brown with a little olive oil. Once browned add the passata and stir with a wooden spoon.
2. Pour in the water, then add the tomato purée, crushed garlic, salt, pepper, half the basil, bay, oregano and chopped chilli.
3. Stir and leave to simmer gently for 3 hours. Twenty minutes before the sugo is ready add the remaining basil and stir.
4. Serve by stirring the sauce through some freshly cooked pasta and enjoy the ribs with a dressed salad.

Carmela's tip

The polpettini di carne from page 80 and the braciole from page 83 can be used in place of the ribs.

Pizza Topping Sauce

Sugo della pizza

This pizza topping sauce is simple yet full of flavour. It can also be used with pasta and is a versatile sauce to have ready made in the fridge.

Preparation time: 5 minutes
Cooking time: 1 hour
Makes: enough for 12 pizzas

680g passata
1 tsp oregano
10 basil leaves, torn
Salt and pepper to season
2 cloves of garlic, peeled and crushed
½ tsp chilli (optional)

1. Put the passata, oregano, basil, salt, pepper, garlic and chilli into a saucepan and simmer for one hour.
2. Once ready set aside and cool until required for your pizza.

Carmela's tip
Any leftover sauce can be kept in the fridge for a week or frozen for up to 6 months.

Roasted Tomato and Pepper Soup

Zuppa di pomodori e poporodle

When vegetables are roasted, they release a certain sweetness and it really does show in this soup. The onions caramelise whilst the peppers and tomatoes burst with their natural sweetness and juices. It's a beautiful and warming soup and freezes well too.

Preparation time: 15 minutes
Cooking time: 60 minutes
Serves: 4

2 red onions, peeled and quartered
4 peppers, quartered
8 large vine tomatoes, halved
4 cloves of garlic, peeled
6 tbsp olive oil
1 litre vegetable stock
Large bunch basil
Small sprig oregano
Salt and pepper

1. Preheat the oven to 180°C (gas 4).
2. Place the onions, peppers, tomatoes and garlic in an ovenproof dish. Season with salt and drizzle over the olive oil.
3. Roast in the oven for 45–55 minutes.
4. Towards the end of the roasting time, pour the stock into a saucepan and begin to warm through.
5. When the vegetables have roasted, place them in a blender along with the stock and blitz for 30 seconds.
6. Taste and season with a little more salt and pepper if needed then add the fresh basil and oregano and blitz again.
7. Pour the soup into a saucepan and warm through for 25 minutes. Season to taste.
8. Serve in warm bowls with rustic bread.

Seasonal Asparagus Pesto

Asparagi salsa

Pesto is every Italian mother's store cupboard essential, quick to toss into pasta, spread over hot bread and drizzle over fish. Asparagus pesto is a little different from the staple basil version and I came up with this recipe whilst using this nutty and robust early summer vegetable.

Preparation time: 5 minutes
Cooking time: 5 minutes
Makes: 250g jar

100g asparagus
50g pine nuts
30g basil
30g Parmesan
Extra virgin olive oil
Salt and pepper

1. Roughly chop the asparagus, then lightly fry in a little olive oil for about 5 minutes or until tender.
2. Once cooked, allow the asparagus to cool, then blitz in a food processor.
3. Into the food processor add the pine nuts, basil and Parmesan, and blitz. Add a little salt and pepper to season.
4. Pour in the olive oil a little at a time until the right consistency is met. You are looking for a soft dropping consistency.

Carmela's tip

Store the pesto in an airtight jar in the fridge and it will keep for 5–7 days.

Simple Tomato Sauce

Sugo di pomodoro

This tasty sauce will make the perfect base for pasta, soups and even pizza toppings. It's simple to prepare and cook, with the added bonus of using store cupboard staples. I tend to make the sauce in bulk and freeze it in batches.

Preparation time: 10 minutes
Cooking time: 1 hour 10 minutes
Serves: 4

4 tbsp olive oil
1 small onion, finely chopped
3 cloves garlic, peeled and finely sliced
1 carrot, finely chopped
1 stick celery, finely chopped
2 tbsp tomato purée
50ml water
2 x 400g tins plum tomatoes
Salt and pepper
Handful basil, torn

1. Pour the olive oil into a saucepan and gently fry off the onion and garlic for 2 minutes.
2. Tumble in the carrot and celery, stir and cook for a further 5 minutes, then squeeze in the tomato purée and mix.
3. Pour in 50ml water and stir, then add the plum tomatoes and season well with salt and pepper.
4. Add half of the basil and cook for 1 hour, ensuring that you stir every 10 minutes so that the sauce doesn't catch on the base of the pan.
5. When the sauce is rich and thickened, add the remaining basil and stir.

Carmela's tip

The sauce can be frozen for up to 6 months or kept in the fridge for a week.

Sundried Tomato Pesto
Pesto alla pomodoro

Fresh and light, with the flavour of the beautiful Mediterranean, pesto adds an instant hit of sunshine to any lunchtime or evening meal. Tomato pesto is very simple to prepare and so versatile, stirred through pasta, on hot bread and as a marinade over chicken, fish or lamb.

Preparation time: 5 minutes
Makes: 200g jar

1 clove of garlic, peeled
25g pine nuts
250g jar of sundried tomatoes; the drained weight is 170g
Big handful of fresh parsley
30g Parmesan, grated
125ml olive oil, plus a little extra for the topping
1 small red chilli, optional

1. Blitz the clove of garlic and pine nuts in the food processor.
2. Tumble in the sundried tomatoes, parsley, Parmesan and chilli, if using. Blitz again as you slowly add the olive oil.
3. Give it all a good mix to the right consistency that would suit you. I like my pesto to still have a little texture to it.
4. Spoon the mixture into sterilized jars and top with a little extra olive oil, seal and pop in the fridge. This pesto will last in the fridge for about 7–10 days.
5. Serve stirred through pasta.

Vegetable Stock

Brodo di verdure

Every cook needs to be able to make a simple stock, whether it is vegetable, chicken or fish stock. It is essential for soups, stews and so many other dishes. Stock can be frozen and this recipe is great to make if you have vegetables lurking in the bottom of the fridge that need to be used up.

Preparation time: 10 minutes
Cooking time: 1 hour
Makes: 1.8 litres

2.5 litres water
1 onion, halved
2 celery sticks (including leafy tops), chopped
2 carrots, peeled and chopped
4 ripe tomatoes, quartered
2 garlic cloves, peeled and halved
Salt and pepper to season

1. Put the water, onion, celery, carrots, tomatoes and garlic in a large saucepan and season with a little salt and pepper.
2. Simmer over a medium heat for 1 hour, stirring occasionally.
3. Once the stock is ready and the vegetables have completely softened, strain the contents of the pan through a sieve and into a clean bowl.
4. Push the vegetables through the sieve with a wooden spoon, as they will still hold lots of flavour and moisture. Scrape off the bottom of the sieve to remove any pulp and stir it into the stock.

Carmela's tip
The stock can be frozen for 6 months or kept in the fridge for 5 days.

Zesty Sauce

Gremolata

Gremolata is traditionally made to go alongside osso buco, however I like to use it whenever and wherever possible. It works very well with braised meats, especially lamb chops.

Preparation time: 5 minutes
Serves: 6

Zest of 2 lemons
100g parsley, finely chopped
2 garlic cloves, peeled and crushed
Pinch of salt
1–2 tbsp olive oil

1. Put the lemon zest, parsley, garlic, salt and olive oil into a bowl and stir well.
3. Serve alongside grilled meat.

Carmela's tip
Stores in the fridge for 3 days.

Gorgonzola Sauce
Salsa al gorgonzola

Gorgonzola sauce is delicate and incredibly versatile and simple to make. I urge any 'blue cheese haters' to try it! This sauce is perfect to accompany potato gnocchi or pasta and makes a quick and speedy dinner. The recipe uses gorgonzola, but dolcelatte also works well.

Preparation time: 10 minutes
Serves: 2

25g butter
1 small white onion, finely chopped
1 garlic clove, finely chopped
50ml double cream
Pepper to season
Pinch grated nutmeg
200g gorgonzola
5 sage leaves, finely chopped
30g Parmesan, grated

1. Place the butter in a sauté pan, add the garlic and chopped onion, and soften gently for 5 minutes until the onion is translucent.
2. Add the cream to the pan and season with a pinch of pepper and grated nutmeg.
3. Crumble in the gorgonzola and stir over a low heat until the cheese has melted, being careful not to burn the sauce. Continue to stir and cook for a further 5 minutes.
4. Add the chopped sage and Parmesan, stir well.
5. Serve with your chosen cooked gnocchi or pasta.

Bread
and Pizza

For an Italian, it's not a meal if there isn't bread on the table, so there is always a small wicker breadbasket present on my dining table. Whether your preference is for a light and fresh fennel bread or a mixed olive loaf, bread is used to dip into the pasta and meat sauces and scrape around the side of the bowl. Food makes memories and I recall that as children my sister and I would love to eat pastina, tiny pasta shapes cooked in a stock. With a large bowl each we would tear up and dunk fresh bread in the stock before taking large, delicious spoonfuls.

My other childhood love was pizza. Master a basic dough, add some favourite toppings and you will have everyone smiling around you. Whether you choose a simple pizza marinara or a plump filled calzone, stone baked is best. Invest in a pizza stone for your oven to get the delicious flavour and texture of a traditional pizza oven, but make sure you preheat it until it is hot to the finger's touch.

When making bread use tepid water (body temperature) to activate the yeast. This will aid the bread's gentle proving and flavour, while hot water would damage the yeast. When proving breads they should be left in a warm place away from draughts, then cook the bread in a preheated oven on a hot pizza stone or upturned baking sheet. By allowing the pizza stone or baking tray to heat this will ensure the bread or pizza has a crispy crust.

Nonna Carmela's Pizza Doughballs

Pitole di Nonna Carmela

Pitole are Nonna Carmela's famous pizza dough balls that she would normally make through the month of December. Anticipation would set in as soon as December began, as pitole are a delicious, light treat. I would over-indulge – as I often do when eating fantastic food. These doughballs can be filled, but as they are fried I think simplicity here will do. Pitole is pizza dough, deep fried in oil, unlike conventional, baked doughballs. Once browned and golden, they are ready to eat. A large batch would normally last a week and could just be reheated in a low oven to soften slightly.

Preparation time: 10 minutes
Proving time: 1 hour
Cooking time: 20 minutes
Makes: 30

7g dried yeast
300ml tepid water
500g '00' flour
5g salt
2 tbsp olive oil
2 litres sunflower oil, for deep frying

1. Mix the yeast with the tepid water and stir.
2. Pour the flour into a large bowl and sprinkle in the salt.
3. Make a well in the centre of the flour and gently pour in the yeasted water. Use your fingertips to mix the ingredients together to form a dough.
4. Turn out onto a lightly floured surface and knead for 8–10 minutes until smooth.
5. Cover and leave to prove for 1 hour.

6. Take a large saucepan and three quarters fill it with sunflower oil. Bring the oil up to cooking temperature – test it by dropping in a teaspoon of dough, and if the dough turns brown and floats to the top then the oil is ready to use.

7. Turn out the proved dough and pull off apple-size pieces. Form the dough into a pear shape by pulling on each end and stretching it.

8. In batches, drop a couple of pitole at a time into the oil. Once they turn golden brown and float turn them over and cook on the underside for a further minute.

9. Remove with a slotted spoon and drain on kitchen towel while you continue to cook the remaining dough.

10. Serve and enjoy.

Carmela's tip

After a few days, if the pitole are a little stale, warm them through for a couple of minutes in a low oven.

Fennel Seed Bread
Pane con finocchietto

Italians embrace fennel from the large, liquorice-flavoured white bulb to the tiny, oval husk seeds, which are sharp, sweet and wonderful with lamb, pork and fresh fish. A raw bulb of fennel can be sliced into a salad or braised with olive oil and thyme with the leafy fennel top chopped and stuffed into a round fish and baked. The seeds add flavour and bite and work well in this bread and the delicate fennel taralle on page 186.

Preparation time: 15 minutes
Proving time: 2 hours 30 minutes
Cooking time: 30–35 minutes
Serves: 6–8

300g strong white flour
150g '00' flour
6g salt
1tbsp fennel seeds, crushed
290ml tepid water
7g dried yeast
20g butter, melted

1. Pour the flour into a large bowl and sprinkle in the salt.
2. Crush the fennel seeds using a pestle and mortar. This will add texture to the bread by varying the size of the fennel seeds.
3. Add the yeast to the tepid water and stir, this will start the action of the yeast.
4. Sprinkle three quarters of the fennel seeds into the flour and slowly pour in the yeasted water and melted butter.
5. Using your fingertips, work the flour and water together until you have the start of a dough. Once combined, tip the dough out onto a lightly floured board.
6. Knead the dough for 8–10 minutes and form the dough into a ball.

7. Place the dough into a clean, oiled bowl and allow to prove for 1 hour 30 minutes in a warm place away from draughts.
8. After the first prove, tip the dough out onto a lightly floured surface. Knock it back by folding repeatedly in on itself using the heels of your hands on a lightly floured surface, form into an oval then leave to prove for a further hour.
9. Preheat the oven to 190°C (gas 5).
10. Place the dough onto an oiled baking tray, slash the top with a sharp knife and sprinkle over the remaining fennel seeds.
11. Bake for 30 minutes until the loaf is golden and sounds hollow when tapped.

Filled Calzone Pizza

Calzone con verdure

Calzone evokes so many memories for me. Meeting my husband 15 years ago he took me to a beautiful quaint Italian restaurant called 'The Italian Job'. They always made us feel incredibly welcome as well as making the most delicious and authentic calzone I have ever tasted. If you don't like pizza, think they are boring or simply cheese on toast then please try a calzone. And if you think there's nothing better than homemade pizza; well a calzone blows it straight out of the Mediterranean! Any flavour combinations work, from peppers and mushrooms to meatballs and chicken with fresh basil pesto. It is a little bit of Italy rolled, filled and dished up with stone-baked casing.

Preparation time: 20 minutes
Cooking time: 12 minutes
Serves: 4

For the dough:
Prepared pizza dough (page 58). You will need half the pizza dough recipe.
For the filling:
2 tbsp olive oil
20 mushrooms, sliced
3 bell peppers, sliced
250g fresh mozzarella, chopped
Handful basil, torn
Salt and pepper to season
One ladle of pizza sauce (page 35)

1. Preheat the oven to 220°C (gas 7).
2. Clean, slice and fry off the mushrooms in a little olive oil until softened and lightly coloured. Try not to overcrowd the pan, as the mushrooms will not colour.
3. Slice the peppers lengthways, place on a baking tray with a drizzle of olive oil and bake for 20 minutes.

4. Mix all the filling ingredients together in a bowl and set aside.
5. Take a ball of pizza dough roughly the size of an orange and roll out to a thin round, the size of a large dinner plate.
6. Spoon some of the filling onto one side of the dough and fold over the remaining dough.
7. Crimp the edges together, like a pasty.
8. Make two small slits in the top of the calzone (so it doesn't go pop in the oven) and tuck in a sage leaf. Bake until lightly golden.
9. Serve with a green salad.

Carmela's tip

To make the perfect glaze, whisk together 1 tbsp of tomato purée and 3 tbsp of olive oil. Using a pastry brush, lightly glaze the calzone before it goes in the oven – perfecto! If you like extra sauce, spoon some warm tomato sugo over the top of the calzone once cooked.

Flat Topped Bread

Focaccia con pomodori secchi e cipolla

Focaccia was the first bread I ever learnt to make. I love the fingertip dents that fill with pools of olive oil. It's a very delicious bread, best eaten on the day it's made, and is perfect to complete a lunch platter of cured meats. The topping flavours can be changed to suit the season and what you have in the larder. Keep it simple using rosemary sprigs, salt and olive oil or make it robust with roasted peppers, olives and thyme.

Preparation time: 25 minutes
Proving time: 2 hours 15 minutes
Cooking time: 20 minutes
Serves: 6

For the dough:
250g strong white flour
250g '00' flour
8g salt
300ml tepid water
7g yeast
4 tbsp olive oil
For the topping:
3 tbsp olive oil
1 small red onion
1 tsp sugar
50g sundried tomatoes, drained and chopped
Sprig rosemary
Olive oil to drizzle
Salt to season

1. Mix both flours and salt together in a large mixing bowl.
2. Add the dried yeast to the tepid water and stir to activate the yeast.
3. Make a well in the centre of the flour and pour in the yeasty water and olive oil.

4. Using your fingertips, combine the flour and liquid to form a dough.
5. Turn the dough out onto a lightly floured surface and knead for 8–10 minutes. The dough should be smooth and elastic. If it is sticky, add a little more flour.
6. Form the dough into a ball and place into a lightly oiled bowl. Cover with a clean tea towel and allow to prove for 1 hour 30 minutes in a warm area of the kitchen away from any draught.
7. Slice the onion, and fry in 3 tbsp of olive oil in a frying pan for 4 minutes.
8. Sprinkle in the sugar, stir and soften the onions for a further 10 minutes, being careful not to burn them.
9. Chop up the sundried tomatoes and set to one side.
10. After the first prove, tip the dough onto an oiled baking tray. Using your fingertips push the dough out so you are leaving dimples impressed into the dough.
11. Sprinkle over the caramelised onions and sundried tomatoes. Cover with cling film and allow to prove for a further 45 minutes while you preheat the oven to 220°C (gas 7).
12. Sprinkle over a little rock salt and drizzle over the olive oil. Bake for 20 minutes until golden.
13. Serve with cured meats.

Carmela's tip

To add flavour to the bread, you can drizzle over the oil from the sundried tomatoes jar instead of olive oil.

Mediterranean Filled Loaf
Stromboli

'Stromboli' bread is a meal in itself. The sweet fruits of the Mediterranean have jumped into this bread and have been rolled up tight before being tucked into bed and baked. It's perfect alongside some cured meats, olives, artichokes and salad, but is also a tasty alternative for a picnic or children's lunchboxes. Stromboli keeps very well due to the moisture of the filling. To re-heat the loaf just pop into a low oven, wrapped in a sheet of parchment paper for five minutes.

Preparation time: 30 minutes
Proving time: 2 hours
Cooking time: 35 minutes
Serves: 6–8

For the dough:
350g strong white flour
4g salt
200ml tepid water
7g dried yeast
3 tbsp olive oil
1 tbsp fresh rosemary, finely chopped
For the filling:
250g mozzarella, chopped
50g Parmesan, grated
150g roasted peppers
3 tbsp basil, torn
1 garlic clove, peeled and crushed
Pepper to season
1 tsp dried oregano
1 small red chilli, finely sliced (optional)

1. Mix the flour and salt together in a large mixing bowl.
2. Add the dried yeast to the tepid water and stir. This will activate the yeast.

3. Make a well in the centre of the flour and pour in the yeasty water and olive oil, then sprinkle over the chopped rosemary.
4. Using your fingertips, combine the flour and liquid to form a dough.
5. Turn the dough out onto a lightly floured surface and knead for 8–10 minutes. The dough should be smooth and elastic. If it is sticky, add a little more flour.
6. Form the dough into a ball and place into a lightly oiled bowl.
7. Cover with a clean tea towel and allow to prove for 1 hour 30 minutes in a warm area of the kitchen away from any draught.
8. Prepare the filling. Into a bowl tumble the chopped mozzarella, grated Parmesan, roasted peppers, basil, garlic, pepper, oregano and chilli. Mix with a fork, cover and set aside.
9. Lightly flour the surface and turn out the dough. Roll the dough to the size of a swiss roll tin around 30 x 25cm.
10. Turn the dough so the shortest side is facing you. Sprinkle over the filling allowing a margin of 1–2cm all the way around.
11. Roll from the shortest side, tucking in the edges as you go.
12. Place onto a baking tray and cover with cling film. Allow to rest for 30 minutes while you preheat the oven to 190°C (gas 5).
13. Bake for 35 minutes until golden.
14. Serve as part of an antipasti starter or with a salad as a light lunch.

Carmela's tip
Parma ham would also be a wonderful additional ingredient.

Olive Bread

Pane di olive

Plump, sun-kissed olives in a wonderfully chewy bread, sliced and topped with salted cured meats, sounds like my ideal antipasti feast. Never buy olives that have already been pitted as they just seem to lose their flavour. Either use a knife and slice the olives from the stone or borrow an olive or cherry stoner – you simply place the olive into the pitter and use it like a nut cracker. Be careful as the stone will fly out at speed. Use a mixture of your favourite olives, from deep ebony black to forest green; these will add texture and a difference in flavour and fragrance to the bread.

Preparation time: 15 minutes
Proving time: 2 hours 30 minutes
Cooking time: 40 minutes
Serves: 6

250g strong white flour
250g '00' flour
6g salt
250ml warm water
7g dried yeast
100g butter, melted
125g olives, halved

1. In a large bowl, mix together the flour and salt.
2. Tip the yeast into the warm water and stir. This will activate the yeast.
3. Make a well in the centre of the flour and gently pour in the water, then combine using your fingertips.
4. Add the butter to the dough and work it through, adding a little more flour if required.
5. Once combined, tip the dough onto a lightly floured surface and knead for 8–10 minutes until the dough is smooth.

6. Place the dough into a lightly oiled bowl and cover with a clean tea towel, then leave to prove for 1 hour 30 minutes in a warm and draught-free place.
7. Prepare and halve the selected olives.
8. Once the dough has proved, tip it out onto a lightly floured board and work in the olives for 2 minutes.
9. Shape the dough into a ball, cover and allow it to prove for a further 60 minutes. If you have a proving basket you can use it now.
10. Preheat the oven to 220°C (gas 7).
11. Once the dough has finished its second prove, transfer it onto a lightly oiled tray and bake until golden and – once tapped on the bottom – the bread sounds hollow.
12. Serve with antipasti.

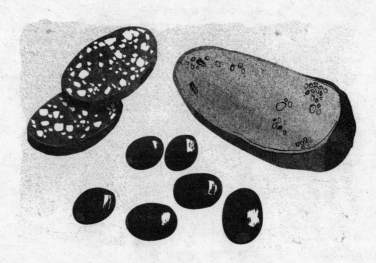

Parmesan Breadsticks

Grissini con parmigiano

A handful of warm bread grissini garnished with some fresh Parma ham and olives makes a very tempting and delicious snack for any time of the day or a lovely nibble at a drinks party.

190ml semi-skimmed milk, warmed
7g dried yeast
300g strong white flour
100g butter, softened
5g salt
Pepper to season
80g freshly grated Parmesan
½ tsp dried marjoram or oregano

1. Preheat the oven to 160°C (gas 3).
2. Heat the milk in the microwave for 30 seconds then add the yeast and stir.
3. Put the flour, butter, salt, pepper, Parmesan and marjoram in a large bowl and then pour in the milk.
4. Stir with a wooden spoon until you form a dough.
5. Transfer the dough to a lightly floured board and knead for about 3 minutes.
6. Roll out with a rolling pin to the thickness of a pound coin. Cut the dough into long lengths, around 1cm wide by 30cm long.
7. Arrange on a greased baking tray and bake for 25 minutes.
8. Serve with antipasti.

Bread Balls

Polpette

If you have stale bread as I often do lurking in the bottom of the bread bin, then these fluffy polpette pillows are perfect to rustle up. They are light, full of flavour and smell amazing too, spiked with garlic and fresh herbs pulled from the garden. Polpette can be eaten both warm and cold and are also delicious dipped in a lovely fresh ragu sauce and served after pasta with a fresh leafy salad. They freeze incredibly well too, once cooked.

Preparation time: 10 minutes
Cooking time: 15 minutes
Serves: 4 (makes about 10 polpette)

120g stale breadcrumbs
55g grated Parmesan
1 tsp bicarbonate of soda
2 cloves garlic, peeled and crushed
4 large eggs
Bunch of fresh parsley; chopped
Salt and pepper
Olive oil to fry

1. Tip the breadcrumbs into a roomy bowl followed by the grated Parmesan, bicarbonate of soda, crushed garlic, eggs and chopped parsley. Mix well and season with salt and pepper.
2. You are looking for a loose mixture but it must be able to hold itself when formed into balls. Shape the bread balls into quenelles using two tablespoons or roll them between your palms to make plump balls.
3. Shallow fry in batches in a frying pan with rapeseed oil until golden brown on all sides.
4. Drain the bread balls on kitchen towel to remove any excess oil.
5. Serve by dipping into a ragu 5 minutes before serving or eat them as they are, warm, with a soup or salad.

Pizza Dough Perfection
Pizza

Naples is famous for the simple, popular and deliciously divine pizza, which is now eaten all over the world. Using a pizza oven produces a stone baked finish and gives the pizza a little something special, but a pizza stone heated in a conventional oven is a good second best. The simplest topping, a margarita – tomato, mozzarella and a leaf of basil – is said to be named after an Italian queen.

Preparation time: 1 hour 20 minutes
Cooking time: 8 minutes per pizza
Makes: 6 large pizzas

900g '00' flour
10g salt
21g dried yeast
550ml tepid water (see note below)
5 tbsp olive oil

1. Tip the yeast into warm water and stir to activate it.
2. Put the flour and salt in a large bowl, make a well in the centre and add the oil.
3. Slowly add the water, a little at a time.
4. Use a wooden spoon initially or use your hands to mix in the water. It may be a little messy to start with.
5. Tip the dough out on to a floured surface and knead for approximately 7–10 minutes or do this in a mixer with a dough hook, which will be quicker. The dough should be soft, smooth and spring back when pushed with the tips of your fingers.

6. Place the dough in a lightly oiled bowl with a little flour on top. Lay a damp tea towel over the bowl and leave in a warm area of the kitchen to prove.
7. The dough will need to prove for at least 1 hour 30 minutes, but the longer you leave it, the better the flavour will be.

Carmela's tip

I use the milky water from bags of fresh mozzarella in place of tap water when making the dough. It's full of flavour and means that there is no waste at all. My mother has been doing this for years and also uses the milk from excess ricotta. If the water or mozzarella milk is warm, the proving will be accelerated, however I recommend tepid water and a slightly longer prove, to allow the flavour to develop in the dough.

Pizza Florentina

Pizza fiorentina

When I make pizza fiorentina, my mother comes to mind immediately. It's her absolute favourite combination of soft spinach with a wonderfully dippy egg centre. It's simple to make and mouth-wateringly full of flavour, but for added heat you could add a little chopped chilli. Served with a rocket salad, this pizza is a little bite of heaven.

Preparation time: 10 minutes
Cooking time: 12 minutes
Makes: 4 pizzas

Pizza dough (half the recipe, page 58)
Pizza sauce (half the recipe, page 35)
30g '00' flour and 20g polenta grain, mixed together, for dusting
2 garlic cloves, peeled and finely sliced
600g spinach, blanched and drained well
250g mozzarella, chopped
Nutmeg, grated
70g Parmesan, grated
4 eggs
Pepper to season

1. Preheat the oven to 220°C (gas 7).
2. Divide the pizza dough into four equal balls then roll out into discs on a surface dusted with the mix of flour and polenta.
3. Evenly spread some tomato sauce over each pizza base.
4. Scatter the sliced garlic, spinach and mozzarella evenly over each pizza base.
5. Grate a little nutmeg over each pizza along with the Parmesan.
6. Cook each pizza in the middle of the oven for 6 minutes.
7. Remove the pizza from the oven and crack an egg into the centre of the pizza, then return to the oven for a further 6 minutes.
8. Serve sliced and with a grind of pepper.

Pizza Marinara

Pizza marinara

The original and first ever Neapolitan pizza, this is my absolute favourite, as it showcases the simplest of ingredients at their best. By simply swapping the garlic and oregano for mozzarella and a little basil you have a margarita.

Preparation time: 20 minutes
Cooking time: 10 minutes per pizza
Makes: 6–8 pizzas

Pizza dough (page 58)
Pizza sauce (page 35)
1 garlic clove, finely sliced
1 tsp dried oregano
30g '00' flour and 20g polenta grain, mixed together, for dusting

1. Preheat the oven and pizza stone to 220°C (gas 7).
2. Divide the dough into 6–8 portions, then roll out into a thin disc on a surface dusted with the flour and polenta mix. Use your hands to gently pull and encourage the dough. If you are feeling confident, throw the dough into the air allowing it to fall onto your fist gently and stretch under its own weight.
3. If you prefer, use a rolling pin until you reach the correct thickness, I like mine to be 1cm in depth.
4. Place the dough gently onto a hot pizza stone. Spread with a ladle of the pizza sauce and sprinkle over the garlic.
5. Scatter over the oregano and bake for 10 minutes until the edge of the pizza is golden.
6. Serve sliced with a rocket and balsamic salad.

Pizza Puttanesca

Pizza puttanesca

A delicious pizza with a somewhat curious name, coined because the ladies of the night were said to feed it to the sailors from the port in Naples. If you like it hot and spicy then pizza puttanesca is the one for you – with salty anchovies and a combination of olives, capers and chilli, it's just perfect.

Preparation time: 10 minutes
Cooking time: 12 minutes
Makes: 4

Pizza dough (half the quantity, page 58)
Pizza sauce (half the quantity, page 35)
20 anchovy fillets
20 black olives, pitted and halved
2 tbsp capers, chopped
1 large red chilli, finely chopped
30g Parmesan, grated
30g parsley, chopped
2 tbsp olive oil
30g '00' flour and 20g polenta grain, mixed together, for dusting

1. Preheat the oven and pizza stone to 220°C (gas 7).
2. Divide the dough into 4 portions. Dust your work surface with the flour and polenta mixture then roll each piece of dough into a thin disc.
3. Use your hands to gently pull and encourage the dough, if you are feeling confident throw the dough into the air allowing it to fall onto your fist gently to stretch under its own weight.
4. If you prefer, use a rolling pin until you reach the correct thickness.

5. Place the dough gently onto a hot pizza stone. Spread with a ladle of the pizza sauce and scatter over the anchovies, olives, capers and chilli.
6. Sprinkle over Parmesan and bake for 10 minutes until the edge of the pizza is golden.
7. Remove from the oven. Scatter over the chopped parsley and drizzle over a little olive oil.
8. Serve sliced with a seasonal leaf salad.

Twisted Bread Sticks with Olive, Parmesan and Oregano

Grissini con olive, parmigiano e oregano

These long, leggy batons of bread are moreish and easy to prepare, and they're perfect wrapped in Parma ham and eaten with other accompaniments or torn and dipped into balsamic vinegar (my favourite). I often make them for the children's lunchboxes and also to go alongside a bowl of warming soup.

Preparation time: 1 hour 15 minutes
Cooking time: 25 minutes
Serves: 6

250g strong white flour
250g '00' flour
8g salt
7g yeast
1 level tsp dried oregano
3 tbsp olive oil (plus a little extra for greasing)
350ml tepid water
70g freshly grated Parmesan
70g black dried olives, quartered

1. Put the flour in a large bowl and stir with a wooden spoon. Make a well in the centre so you can see the bottom of the bowl.
2. Sprinkle the salt into one side of the bowl and the yeast into the other side, keeping them separate. Add the oregano and olive oil.
3. Gently pour in the water and, using a wooden spoon or your hands, form the mixture into a workable dough.
4. Sprinkle some '00' flour onto the work surface and turn out the dough. Knead well for 8 minutes until the dough is smooth and springs back.

5. Place the dough in a lightly oiled bowl, cover with a clean tea towel and allow to prove for 60 minutes.
6. Preheat the oven to 200°C (gas 6) and grease two baking trays with a little olive oil.
7. Leaving the dough in the bowl, add the grated Parmesan and the olives.
8. Fold the dough to incorporate the Parmesan and olives, then turn it out onto a lightly floured surface and continue to fold to ensure all of the Parmesan and olives are combined well into the dough.
9. Flatten the dough and cut into 15 strips.
10. Stretch and roll each strip of dough to the desired length (the length of the baking tray).
11. Repeat until you have used all the dough. Cover and allow to prove for 20 minutes, then bake for 25 minutes until golden.
12. Serve as part of an antipasti platter or alongside a delicious roasted red pepper soup.

Carmela's tip

Try to use a mixture of different olives to add a variation of colour, taste and texture.

Semolina Bread

Pane pugliese

A robust bread, which takes little effort to make and requires only staple ingredients from your store cupboard. Semolina flour is found in every kitchen from the north to the south of Italy. This bread is best eaten fresh on the day it's made, although after a few days it's perfect to make panzanella salad.

Preparation time: 15 minutes
Proving time: 2 hours 30 minutes
Cooking time: 20 minutes
Serves: 6

365g strong white flour
150g fine semolina
8g salt
330ml tepid water
7g fast action yeast

1. Put the flour and semolina in a large bowl, add the salt and make a well in the centre of the flour.
2. Add the yeast to the tepid water and stir to activate, then slowly add the yeasty water to the flour.
3. Using the tips of your fingers combine the flour mixture into a ball of dough.
4. Sprinkle a board with a little semolina and turn the dough out.
5. Knead for 8-10 minutes until smooth then place in a lightly oiled bowl and prove for 1 hour 30 minutes in a warm place, away from draughts.
6. Knock the dough back and split it into two equal loaves. Roll into two balls.
7. Place onto an oiled baking tray and sprinkle with a little semolina then leave to prove for a further 1 hour in a warm place away from draughts.
8. Preheat the oven to 180°C (gas 4).
9. Use a sharp knife to score the top of each loaf then bake for 25 minutes until golden in colour.

Meat, Poultry and Game

Veal, lamb, pork or the humble chicken in a slowly cooked, tender stew with softened mouth-watering vegetables provide a comforting, warming meal as autumn arrives and the winter nights draw in. Game is in keeping with the *cucina povera* style because it often costs nothing if you can catch it yourself. I grew up on a farm where there were often pheasants hanging by their skinny legs in our garage and they and rabbits were skinned in the outside porch before my mother would allow them in the house. If you don't like game, stick with the more traditional meats – the results will be just as delicious.

Beef Steak in Tomato Sauce

Bistecche alla pizzaiola

Bistecche alla pizzaiola is a dish full of memories. Cooking is started off on the stove and then finished slowly in the oven, and the oven dish that I remember from my childhood was 1970s style: white, with small orange flowers on the side. My mum would place the entire dish in the centre of the table with some uncut bread and a leafy salad – a perfect meal to *fare la scarpetta*, or use the bread to mop up and absorb the silky smooth sauce.

Preparation time: 10 minutes
Cooking time: 45 minutes
Serves: 4

5 tbsp olive oil
4 thin rump steaks, 200g per steak
2 garlic cloves, peeled and sliced
3 anchovy fillets, drained
25g capers, drained and chopped
2 x 400g chopped tomatoes
1 tsp dried oregano
1 small red chilli, finely sliced
Handful of basil, chopped
Salt and pepper to season

1. Preheat the oven to 180°C (gas 4).
2. Heat the oil in a large shallow frying pan and fry the steaks for 2 minutes on each side. You may need to do this in batches.
3. Remove the steaks from the pan and set aside.
4. Add the garlic, anchovies and capers, stir well and cook for 2 minutes.
5. Pour in the tinned tomatoes and stir. Sprinkle in the oregano, chilli and half of the chopped basil. Stir again and return the steaks to the pan.
6. Cover the steaks with the tomatoes and season with salt and pepper.
7. Transfer to the oven for 40 minutes. Once cooked, sprinkle on the remaining basil and serve with a leafy salad and bread.

Hunter's Chicken

Pollo cacciatore

Succulent chicken coated in a deep-bodied tomato sauce is a hearty dish for a weary hunter, but it makes a delicious light meal when accompanied with a baby leaf salad and homemade ciabatta. An alternative to using white wine is dry white vermouth, an invaluable store cupboard ingredient in Italian cooking.

Preparation time: 15 minutes
Cooking time: 1 hour 15 minutes
Serves: 6

3 tbsp olive oil
2 cloves garlic, peeled and crushed
2 shallots, sliced
6 chicken breasts
1 large glass white wine
2 x 680g jars passata
1 tsp capers, chopped
100g pitted green olives, halved
2 red peppers, sliced
Salt and pepper to season
1 bay leaf
Handful of basil, chopped
1 tsp fresh oregano

1. Preheat the oven to 180°C (gas 4).
2. Take a large shallow dish and place it on the hob. Lightly fry the shallots and garlic in a little olive oil for 4–5 minutes.
3. Take the chicken breasts and sear on each side with the shallots and garlic.
4. Pour in the white wine and cook for 3 minutes.
5. Add the passata and tumble in the capers, olives, sliced peppers and seasonings.
6. Clamp on the lid and place into the preheated oven for 1 hour 15 minutes.
7. Serve with mashed potatoes or a salad.

Breaded Chicken Cutlets
Cotolette di pollo

Cotolette are thin pieces of meat, dipped in egg and coated in seasoned breadcrumbs. Mine are a little different because I also use polenta in the breadcrumb mix, which adds a delicious crunch on every bite. We would often have cotolette with a salad after a small pasta dish, generally on a Sunday when the family comes together. It really is one of my favourite dishes.

Preparation time: 10 minutes
Cooking time: 25 minutes
Serves: 4

230g dried breadcrumbs
100g grated fresh Parmesan
2 tsp dried tarragon
1 lemon, zest
70g polenta grain
½ tsp chilli flakes (optional)
Salt and pepper to season
Small bunch parsley, chopped
3 large chicken breasts
2 large eggs, beaten
4 tbsp rapeseed oil to shallow fry

1. In a bowl place the breadcrumbs, Parmesan, tarragon, zest, polenta, chilli, salt, pepper and finely chopped parsley. Give all the ingredients a mix and set aside.
2. Take each chicken breast and slice it horizontally. Place the chicken breast on a board and, with one hand securely on top holding the breast down, slide the knife through the breast. You should get three slices out of a large chicken breast.
3. Dip each chicken piece into the beaten egg, then into the breadcrumb and Parmesan mixture. Pat the chicken to ensure it is covered well.

4. To fry, heat the oil in a deep frying pan and cook each cotoletta until golden. They will only need around 3 minutes on one side and a further 2 minutes on the other side. Cook in batches and do not overcrowd the pan.
5. Once the chicken is ready, place each piece onto kitchen towel to remove any excess grease, cover with foil and place in a warm oven until the chicken is ready to serve.
6. Serve warm with a lemon wedge and salad. Any leftovers are delicious cold in sandwiches.

Carmela's tip

To make the cotolette I use chicken breasts sliced and beaten out, with a rolling pin or mallet, but pork escalopes work really well too; you need 6 for this recipe.

Braised Rabbit with White Wine and Fresh Herbs

Coniglio con vino bianco

Rabbit is still not used enough in the kitchen, but it is an inexpensive and very delicious meat that works well in a tomato-based sauce, roasted, stuffed and sautéed in white wine. Ask your butcher to clean, prepare and joint the rabbit if you don't feel confident to do it yourself.

Preparation time: 10 minutes
Cooking time: 1 hour 20 minutes
Serves: 4

5 tbsp olive oil
1 garlic clove, crushed
1 small onion, sliced
1 rabbit, jointed
2 glasses white wine
Sprig rosemary
500g tomatoes, peeled and chopped
Salt and pepper to season
250ml vegetable stock
3 tbsp basil, chopped
1 small red chilli, finely sliced

1. Heat the oil in a large pan over a medium heat.
2. Add the garlic and onion to the pan and gently fry off for 5 minutes.
3. Gently add the rabbit pieces to the pan and sauté until browned on both sides.
4. Pour over the white wine, add the rosemary sprig and stir. Cook for around 5 minutes over a medium heat to reduce the white wine.
5. Tumble in the chopped tomatoes and season with salt and pepper.

6. Pour in half the vegetable stock and reserve the remaining for later, if required.
7. Stir and scatter over the basil and slivers of sliced chilli.
8. Cover, reduce the heat and cook for 1 hour. Check from time to time and, if the pan has become a little dry, add a little more of the reserved stock.
9. Serve immediately with rustic bread and seasonal vegetables.

Carmela's tip

To remove the skins from the tomatoes, make a cross on the bottom of each tomato and plunge into boiling water for 2 minutes. Then drain and plunge into cold water. This will make the tomatoes easy to peel.

Breaded Veal with Tomato Salad

Vitello scallopine con salata di pomodori

The flavour of veal is sweet and very delicate and is best showcased with simple cooking and lightly flavoured sauces. I like to serve vitello scallopine with a plum tomato salad and a squeeze of zesty lemon – very delicious. If you are struggling to find veal then use pork escalopes instead.

Preparation time: 10 minutes
Cooking time: 20 minutes
Serves: 6

130g breadcrumbs
20g polenta
30g Parmesan, grated
6 veal escalopes
2 eggs, beaten and seasoned with salt and pepper
30g butter
6 tbsp olive oil
8 plum tomatoes, quartered
Small bunch basil, chopped
¼ tsp dried oregano

1. Put the breadcrumbs, polenta and Parmesan in a bowl and stir to combine.
2. Dip each escalope into the beaten egg then into the breadcrumb mix.
3. Heat the butter in a frying pan along with 2 tbsp of oil. Fry the escalopes until they are golden on each side, then drain on kitchen towel to absorb any excess oil.
4. Into a bowl tip the tomatoes along with the basil and drizzle over the remaining olive oil. Season with salt and a little pepper. Sprinkle in the oregano and stir.
5. Serve the tomato salad over the veal escalope with an extra drizzle of olive oil and a wedge of lemon.

Lamb, Pea and Egg Bake

Spezzatiello con piselli

Here is a variation of spezzatiello, this time using peas from the freezer. However, if fresh peas are in season then get podding. A little work and preparation on the stove and a final bake in the oven leaves the lamb soft and tender. This is one of my family's favourite *cucina povera* recipes – delicious served with a little rustic bread.

Preparation time: 20 minutes
Cooking time: 2 hours
Serves: 4

500g lamb neck, cubed
4 tbsp olive oil
1 litre chicken stock
2 small sticks celery
2 tbsp basil, chopped
1 tbsp parsley, chopped
Pepper to season
450g peas
35g Parmesan, grated
6 large eggs

1. Preheat the oven to 190°C (gas 5).
2. Trim any fat off the lamb and cut it into bite-sized pieces.
3. Add the oil to a saucepan and place over a medium heat. Fry the lamb on a gentle heat for 10 minutes until the meat is sealed.
4. Slowly pour in the chicken stock then add the celery, basil, parsley and pepper and stir well. Cook on a medium heat for 30 minutes.
5. Scatter in the peas and stir, then continue to cook for a further 10 minutes.
6. In a bowl, whisk together the Parmesan and eggs.
7. Pour three quarters of the egg mixture into the lamb and stir well. Let this bubble for 10 minutes to cook the eggs.
8. Tip the lamb mixture into an ovenproof dish, top with the remaining egg mixture and place in the preheated oven for 50-60 minutes until golden brown.
9. Serve in a warm bowl.

Liver and Onions
Fegato con cipolla

Offal is inexpensive and was used often in our home when I was growing up, offered to us children as a delicious smooth pâté or slow cooked with a deep, rich, thickened sauce. This is a wonderful dish to cook as winter approaches and evening meals become warm and comforting.

Preparation time: 10 minutes
Cooking time: 35 minutes
Serves: 4

350g lambs liver
2 tbsp flour, seasoned with salt and pepper
Olive oil
25g butter
1 red onion, sliced
1 white onion, sliced
2 cloves of garlic, sliced
1 tbsp tomato purée
200ml red wine
500ml beef stock
Salt and pepper to season
5 sage leaves, sliced and extra to garnish

1. Trim off any fat or sinew from the liver, then toss the pieces in seasoned flour and flash fry for one minute on each side. This will just sear the liver and encase the flavour. Remove from the pan and set aside to rest while you prepare the sauce.
2. In the same pan now add a glug of olive oil and 25g of butter. Fry off the sliced onions and garlic, cook for 5 minutes slowly until lightly caramelised. Squeeze in the tomato purée and stir.
3. Pour the red wine into the onions and reduce by half and cook for about 7 minutes.

4. Now add the beef stock, stir and season with salt and pepper. If you like a little added heat then add a pinch of chilli.
5. Place the liver back into the pan and sprinkle the fresh chopped sage over the top. Cook on a medium heat for 20 minutes, until the sauce has thickened slightly.
6. Serve on a bed of lightly seasoned polenta.

Lamb and Escarole Bake
U'Verdette spezzatiello con escarole

Spezzatiello is a traditional Easter dish in the southern Italian region of Puglia. It uses a vegetable leaf called escarole, which is similar to kale or spinach, along with diced lamb, eggs, chicken stock and Parmesan. My parents used to go out foraging with my Nonno Giuseppe and Nonna Carmela picking dandelion leaves, which would be used instead of escarole to make this dish.

Preparation time: 15 minutes
Cooking time: 2 hours
Serves: 4

400g lamb diced
300g blanched escarole, kale or spinach
1.25–1.5 litres chicken stock (or enough to cover the diced lamb in the pan)
6 free range eggs, whisked
100g Parmesan or pecorino, grated
Pepper to season

1. Preheat the oven to 190°C (gas 5).
2. In a saucepan, heat a little olive oil and brown off the diced lamb.
3. Place the blanched escarole into a colander to remove any excess water.
4. Once the lamb has browned, cover with the chicken stock and gently simmer until tender for 1 hour.
5. Whisk the eggs in a bowl and add a little pepper. Add the Parmesan and stir, then set aside.
6. When the lamb has had an hour's cooking, add the escarole and stir. Cook for 10 minutes and then add three quarters of the egg and cheese mixture and stir. Cook for a further 5 minutes until you can see the egg is combining and has become slightly scrambled.

7. Now pour the mixture into an ovenproof dish. Spoon the remaining egg over the top of the spezzatiello and bake for 1 hour until golden.
8. Serve in a warm bowl.

Carmela's tip

Dandelion leaves are full of flavour and have a slightly bitter taste to them. When I was growing up, dandelion leaves would have been used when escarole couldn't be found, and Nonna Carmela still makes spezzatiello with dandelion leaves today.

Meatballs

Polpettini di carne

Freshly made meatballs slowly cooked in a passata tomato sauce is my ideal family meal, served 'Lady and the Tramp' style as a large sharing bowl of meatballs in the centre of the table. Traditionally meatballs are served with polenta, however I do like the long, leggy spaghetti or bucatini too.

Preparation time: 30 minutes
Cooking time: 30 minutes
Serves: 6 (makes around 30 meatballs)

250g minced beef
250g minced pork
1 large egg
40g breadcrumbs
Salt and pepper to season
Small bunch of parsley, chopped
2 garlic cloves, peeled and crushed
1 tsp dried oregano
1 tsp dried chilli
Olive oil, for frying

1. In a bowl, mix together the mince, egg, breadcrumbs, salt, pepper, parsley, garlic, oregano and chilli. You can use a wooden spoon, but I like to use my hands.
2. When the ingredients are all well combined, take a little at a time and roll small, walnut-sized meatballs between your hands. Place them on a plate until you have used up all the mixture.
3. Take a large frying pan and heat a little olive oil. Fry the meatballs in batches until golden brown all over, then remove from the pan and drain on kitchen towel to absorb any excess oil.
5. Serve on a bed of polenta with a little tomato sauce.

Carmela's tip

Make extra to freeze. Lay the meatballs on a tray and place in the freezer until they are almost frozen, then transfer them to a food bag, seal and date. This will help to prevent the meatballs all freezing together into one mass.

Roasted Pheasant with Pancetta and White Wine

Arrosto di fagiano con pancetta e vino bianco

Whilst growing up on a farm in the countryside, my father would become excited in anticipation of the autumn pheasant season. Off he would go into the dark of the night and normally come home holding one or two pheasant by their skinny legs, extremely proud of himself, the hunter! This delicious roast is the perfect way to serve a pheasant – it's a great alternative to chicken.

Preparation time: 15 minutes
Cooking time: 1 hour 30 minutes
Serves: 4

1 sprig rosemary
1 sprig thyme
4 tbsp olive oil
1 lemon, zested and quartered
1 garlic clove, peeled and crushed
Salt and pepper to season
1 x 1kg pheasant, cleaned
6 slices pancetta
225ml white wine

1. Preheat the oven to 180°C (gas 4).
2. Chop the rosemary and thyme and place in a small bowl. Pour in the olive oil, and add the zest of the lemon, crushed garlic and a little salt and pepper. Mix well and leave to infuse for 10 minutes.
3. Place the pheasant in a large roasting tin then massage the infused oil over the bird, including the breasts and legs.
4. Insert the quartered lemon segments into the cavity of the bird.
5. Cover the breasts of the pheasant with the slices of pancetta and pour the white wine into the roasting tin.
6. Roast the bird for 1 hour then lower the heat to 160°C (gas 3) for the final 30 minutes. Remember to baste every 10 minutes or so.
7. Check the pheasant is cooked by piercing the thigh – the juices should run clear and the bird should be tender.
8. Allow the pheasant to rest for 15 minutes before carving. Serve with Italian potatoes.

Pan-fried Offal and Pork
Soffrito di Mamma

Soffritto is made using lamb's offal as well as diced cubes of pork. This dish would normally be prepared for lunch by my mother, as a quick snack with some rustic bread, and is still very much loved by all the men in our family. The chilli heat is optional as my father Rocco likes it 'molto caldo', however just omit the chilli if you would prefer a slightly lighter, less punchy taste.

Preparation time: 5 minutes
Cooking time: 20 minutes
Serves: 2–4

200g pork, diced
3 tbsp olive oil
3 lamb's livers, cubed
3 lamb's kidneys, cubed
Pinch of salt
1 small chilli, sliced
Jar of roasted peppers in vinegar; use only 3 peppers sliced
    with 2 tbsp of the vinegar

1. Chop the pork into bite-sized pieces.
2. In a frying pan heat a glug of olive oil and add the pork. Cook for around 10 minutes.
3. Once the pork is almost cooked add the cubed liver and kidneys. Season with salt and scatter over the sliced chilli.
4. Two minutes before serving add 3 peppers from the jar, sliced lengthways, and 2 tbsp vinegar from the pepper jar.
5. Cook for a final 2 minutes, then serve with rustic bread.

Rolled Pork Escalope
Braciole di maiale

A simple dish, made with inexpensive but tender pork. I prefer to slow cook the braciole in a simple tomato sauce, maximising flavour and depth. Serve them after a pasta dish with a salad, or simply with potatoes and greens. For special occasions, add a spoonful of ricotta in the centre of the escalope and then roll and cook – it's simply mouth-watering.

Preparation time: 20 minutes
Cooking time: 3 hours
Serves: 6

12 pork escalopes
Large bunch of fresh basil, torn
4 cloves garlic, peeled and crushed
Salt and pepper to season
1 heaped tsp oregano
1 tsp dried chilli (optional)
Olive oil
Pre-made tomato passata sauce (sugo) page 38

1. Lay the pork escalopes on a board and season with salt and pepper. If they are thick, lay a sheet of cling film over the escalopes and gently pound with a rolling pin.
2. Spread some crushed garlic over each of the pork escalopes and sprinkle on a little of the oregano and chilli.
3. Place two basil leaves on each escalope and roll it up, starting from one of the short ends. Use a cocktail stick to secure the finished roll.
4. When the pork escalopes have all been rolled, place them on a plate.
5. Heat a little olive oil in a frying pan and brown the pork in batches until the rolls are lightly coloured and seared.
6. Once browned, add the braciole to a sugo and cook slowly for 3 hours until tender.

Carmela's tip
For variation, you can also use and roll thin beef steaks or veal instead of the pork.

Pork Stew

Ciambotta

Ciambotta is a traditional Italian stove-top stew. Even to say the word will have Italians hankering over a warming winter bowlful. You can use pork or a soft Italian sausage, accompanied by a large loaf of bread and a glass of wine on the side. If the children are eating this too then be steady with the chilli.

Preparation time: 15 minutes
Cooking time: 1 hour 50 minutes
Serves: 4

Olive oil
1 large onion, sliced
3 cloves garlic, peeled and crushed
800g diced pork, large chunks
2 x 400g tin plum tomatoes
2 tbsp tomato purée
Salt and pepper to season
1 heaped tsp dried oregano
1 large handful of basil, torn
1 small chilli, chopped
300ml water
6 small potatoes peeled and halved
1 medium yellow pepper, diced
10 mushrooms, sliced
1 courgette, cut into chunky slices

1. Fry the onion for 5 minutes until lightly coloured in a saucepan with a generous glug of olive oil.
2. Add the crushed garlic and stir, followed by the diced pork. Stir well and lightly sear the pork for 5 minutes.
3. Pour the tomatoes into a separate bowl and add the tomato purée, salt and pepper, oregano, chopped basil and chilli. Mix well.

4. When the pork has browned pour in the tomato mix and stir, then the water and mix again.
5. Now tip in the potato halves and cook slowly over a low heat for an hour.
6. After the hour's cooking, taste for seasoning and add a little more if required.
7. Now add the peppers, mushrooms and courgettes and cook slowly for a further 35-40 minutes on a low heat until the sauce has thickened and the courgette and pepper have softened.
8. Serve in warm bowls with a basket of bread.

Rabbit with Tomatoes and Olives

Coniglio alla cacciatora

Alla cacciatora – hunter style, with tomatoes – is one of my favourite ways of cooking. Using staple ingredients from the kitchen store cupboard you can easily create a fabulous simple yet flavoursome dish using either chicken, beef or rabbit. Nonna has always been very fond of cooking with rabbit and this is her favourite rabbit dish.

Preparation time: 15 minutes
Cooking time: 1 hour 30 minutes
Serves: 4

5 tbsp olive oil
2 garlic cloves, sliced
2 red onions, sliced
2 rabbits, cleaned and jointed
125ml red wine
750g tinned plum tomatoes
200ml vegetable stock
75g olives, halved
1 sprig rosemary
1 sprig thyme
1 tsp fresh oregano
Salt and pepper to season

1. Heat the olive oil in a large pan, add the garlic and onion and fry gently for 5 minutes.
2. Add the rabbit pieces in batches and brown them off.
3. Once the rabbit is ready return all the pieces to the pan and pour in the wine.
4. Reduce the wine for 5 minutes then tip in the tomatoes and break them up with a wooden spoon.
5. Pour in the stock, olives, herbs and season with salt and pepper. Stir well and clamp on a lid with a little gap to allow the steam to escape.
5. Simmer for 1 hour. Taste and check for seasoning, then serve with polenta.

Zia Maria's Italian Meatloaf
Polpettone

Zia Maria has huge enthusiasm when in the kitchen. She loves nothing more than putting on her apron and spending a morning cooking and baking and sharing her knowledge, experience and ideas. Here is Zia's famous and very much loved Italian meatloaf.

Preparation time: 15 minutes
Cooking time: 1 hour
Serves: 6

300g minced beef
200g minced pork
150g cooked Parma ham, finely sliced
2 cloves garlic, crushed
1 large egg
100g Parmesan, grated
100g fresh breadcrumbs
1 tsp dried oregano
Small bunch parsley, chopped
Small bunch basil, chopped
Salt and pepper to season
Olive oil
100ml water
1 large glass white wine
10 small potatoes, peeled and halved

1. Preheat the oven to 190°C (gas 5).
2. Put the mince in a large bowl and add the Parma ham, garlic, egg, Parmesan and breadcrumbs. Add the oregano, chopped parsley and basil and season with salt and pepper.
3. Use a wooden spoon to mix all the ingredients together, though I prefer to use my hands. Turn the mixture out onto the work surface and shape it into a large sausage.
4. Heat a little olive oil in a frying pan and seal the meatloaf for two minutes on each side.

5. Transfer the meatloaf to an ovenproof dish and pour in the water and white wine.
6. Add the halved potatoes around the meatloaf and season them with salt.
7. Bake in the oven for an hour until golden. Baste every 10 minutes to keep the meatloaf moist.
8. Serve with seasonal vegetables.

Fish and Seafood

Fresh fish and seafood are in abundance on the coastal shores of Italy. The variety is endless: leggy octopi, clams, mussels, eels, squid, red mullet and many more. The fish markets are full of friendly, loud fish sellers and table upon table of freshly caught seasonal fish. If you're fortunate enough to have a local fishmonger you'll get great quality and variety from them, otherwise supermarkets will be your best alternative. If you like your fish with fins try baked bream with capers and lemon or red mullet with olives and thyme. For the more adventurous among you, mussels in tomato sauce, filled calamari or octopus salad may take your fancy.

Baby Octopus Salad
Insalata di polipini

Polpi (octopus) amaze me, from their robust bodies through to their delicate long legs with amazing tiny deep pink suckers. Walking through the markets of Southern Italy you will find various sizes of octopi from the very large and tough variety to the small and delicate polpini, which are equally delicious cooked quickly and served in a salad or bubbled away slowly in a tomato sugo.

Preparation time: 15 minutes
Cooking time: 15 minutes
Serves: 4

2 tbsp red wine vinegar
1 bay leaf
4 small octopi, cleaned
6 small calamari, cleaned and sliced
1 lemon, zest and juice
120ml extra virgin olive oil
Salt and pepper
¼ tsp dried chilli
3 celery sticks, finely sliced
Leaves from celery, finely sliced
Small bunch parsley, chopped

1. Put the vinegar and bay leaf in a saucepan and bring to the boil.
2. Tip in the tiny octopi and sliced calamari and cook for 12–15 minutes. Set the pan aside and allow the polpini to cool.
3. In a bowl, mix the zest and juice of the lemon with the olive oil and season with salt and pepper.
4. Cut the octopi into sections, slice the body into strips and separate the legs.

5. Add the octopi and calamari to the dressing and toss well. Season with salt, pepper and a little chilli, to taste.
6. Toss the seafood with the prepared celery, celery leaves and parsley.

Carmela's tip

If you cannot source fresh octopi and squid then use good quality ones from the freezer, just ensure they have been thoroughly defrosted before use.

Baked Red Mullet

Triglie al forno

The punchy aroma of this dish while cooking is enough to rumble any tummy. Ask your fishmonger to clean the fish for you; they should be soft to touch and the delicate red skin should not be broken or damaged.

Preparation time: 15 minutes
Cooking time: 20 minutes
Serves: 4

Small bunch parsley, roughly chopped
120g black olives, pitted and halved
3 garlic cloves, crushed
1 sprig oregano
1 sprig thyme
1 tsp capers, chopped
6 tbsp olive oil
1 red chilli, finely chopped
1 lemon, juiced
Salt and pepper to season
4 red mullet, cleaned
2 bay leaves

1. Preheat the oven to 190°C (gas 5).
2. In a large bowl, mix together the parsley, olives, garlic, oregano, thyme, capers, olive oil, chilli, lemon juice and season with salt and pepper.
3. Spoon the mixture into the body cavitiy of each fish and lay them in an ovenproof dish.
4. Drizzle with a little more olive oil and place the two bay leaves on top.
5. Bake in the oven for 20 minutes, then serve with steamed spinach, chard or kale.

Baked Sea Bream Parcel
Orata al cartoccio

Sea bream is a very popular fish in the south of Italy. Look out for shiny eyes and healthy gills when you are buying fish – fish should not smell pungent and off-putting but just echo the aroma of the salty sea. Keep this dish light with a salad or add steamed vegetables and potatoes for a winter warmer.

Preparation time: 10 minutes
Cooking time: 25 minutes
Serves: 4

4 tbsp olive oil
2 shallots, finely sliced
2 garlic cloves, sliced
1 tbsp capers, chopped
15 cherry tomatoes, quartered
Small bunch basil, chopped
1 tbsp fresh thyme
1 sprig rosemary, finely chopped
1 large lemon, sliced
4 sea bream, cleaned

1. Preheat the oven to 190°C (gas 5).
2. Mix together in a bowl the olive oil, shallots, garlic, capers, cherry tomatoes, basil, thyme, rosemary and sliced lemon.
3. Fill each bream with the mixture.
4. Take a piece of baking parchment (30cm x 50cm) and fold it in half. Place one of the filled bream in the centre and add a spoonful more of the mixture on top with a little olive oil. Fold the parchment to make a bag and crimp the edges to seal.
5. Repeat with the remaining bream and place them in a baking dish. Bake for 20 minutes until cooked through.
6. Serve with steamed spinach and bread.

Eel in a Tomato Sauce

Anuille con pomodori e vino rosso

This is a recipe that we would prepare for my father, normally at Christmas time and often as a second fish course on Christmas Eve. It's a simple way of cooking this very delicious, snake-like fish. Add chilli for a little warmth or even some chopped seasonal mushrooms to the tomato sauce to make this dish a more substantial main course. I love to serve eel with polenta and lots of bread.

Preparation time: 10 minutes
Cooking time: 1 hour
Serves: 4

4 tbsp olive oil
1 large onion, sliced
2 garlic cloves, sliced
175ml red wine
1 x 400g tinned plum tomatoes
400ml water
2 tbsp tomato purée
3 tbsp parsley, chopped
2 tbsp basil, chopped
800g eel, cleaned and skinned
Salt and pepper to season

1. Preheat the oven to 180°C (gas 4).
2. Pour the olive oil into a large saucepan along with the onion and garlic. Cook on a low heat for 5 minutes until the onions have softened.
3. Pour in the wine and reduce for 3 minutes on a medium heat, stirring.
4. Add the tomatoes, water, tomato purée, parsley and basil. Break the tomatoes down with the back of the wooden spoon and cook for 5 minutes.
5. Add the eel to the pan and cover with the tomatoes. Season with salt and pepper and place in the oven for 50 minutes to cook.
6. Serve with polenta.

Roast Eel with Breadcrumbs
Anguille arroto

Also known as the water snake, eels are eaten all over Italy. As children we were never brave enough to try the fish. I think that was because I remember Nonna wrestling with a large eel in her kitchen sink, then seeing them in the bath – some can reach an unbelievable metre in length – I can't seem to shift that memory to this day!

Preparation time: 10 minutes
Cooking time: 45 minutes
Serves: 4

200g fresh breadcrumbs
2 cloves garlic, crushed
½ tsp chilli
2 tbsp fresh parsley, chopped
½ tsp dried oregano
40g Parmesan, grated
3 tbsp olive oil
Salt and pepper to season
600g eel, cleaned and skin removed
2 bay leaves

1. Preheat the oven to 180°C (gas 4).
2. In a large bowl mix together the fresh breadcrumbs, crushed garlic, chilli, parsley, oregano and Parmesan.
3. Pour in the olive oil and stir the breadcrumb mix. Season with salt and pepper and set aside.
4. Cut the eel into 8cm slices and place in an ovenproof dish.
5. Drizzle over a little olive oil and add the breadcrumbs to the top of the eel, patting down to ensure that the eel is completely covered. Place the 2 bay leaves on top.
6. Bake in the oven for 45 minutes until the breadcrumbs have become golden and the eel is tender and cooked through.
7. Serve with a tomato salad and plenty of bread.

Filled Calamari in a Tomato Sauce

Calamari ripiene con pomodoro

A glorious taste of early summer – calamari has a light flavour and works brilliantly with punchy chilli and other marinades. Whether the calamari is fresh or just thawed from frozen, it should be ivory white and glossy. Ensure that your bread basket is full, as you will need lots of bread to scrape the bowl.

Preparation time: 15 minutes
Cooking time: 45 minutes
Serves: 4

For the sauce:
3 tbsp olive oil
2 cloves garlic, peeled and sliced
800g tinned chopped tomatoes
Salt and pepper to season
10 leaves of basil, torn
For the calamari:
350g cleaned weight calamari, plus tentacles
200g breadcrumbs
2 cloves garlic, peeled and crushed
½ tsp bicarbonate of soda
Small bunch parsley, chopped
½ tsp chilli flakes
2 large eggs
Tentacles from the calamari, chopped into small pieces

1. Start by preparing the sauce. In a large frying pan add the olive oil and sliced garlic. Stir and cook slowly for 2 minutes.
2. Add the chopped tomatoes and stir well. Season with a little salt and pepper and add the torn basil. Leave to simmer while you prepare the calamari.
3. Sprinkle the fresh breadcrumbs into a bowl together with the crushed garlic, bicarbonate of soda, chopped parsley, chopped chilli and eggs.

4. Stir until all the ingredients are well mixed then add the chopped tentacles and mix again.
5. Spoon the mixture into the cleaned calamari body. Leave a little room and secure the top of the calamari with a cocktail stick. Repeat with the remaining calamari.
6. Place the calamari into the frying pan and spoon the tomato sauce over them. Leave them to cook on a medium heat for 1 hour.
7. Serve with rustic bread.

Filled Mussels

Cozze ripiene

Seafood and shellfish are incredibly quick and simple to prepare and cook – just a handful of store cupboard ingredients is enough to make a feast of fresh seafood. A favourite in our home is cozze ripiene, which uses a simple breadcrumb mix to fill juicy and flavoursome mussels.

Preparation time: 20 minutes
Cooking time: 20 minutes
Serves: 4

For the mussels:
12–15 medium mussels
1 glass white wine
For the filling:
4 tbsp extra virgin olive oil
4 anchovy fillets, sliced
1 garlic clove, crushed
1 small chilli, finely chopped
1 tbsp capers, chopped
½ lemon, zest only
30g stale bread, crumbed
Salt and pepper
Small bunch parsley, chopped

1. Preheat the oven to 200°C (gas 6).
2. Clean the mussels by washing them well under cold water. Scrub and shake them, then place in a colander to drain. Remove any beards by pulling them off gently and knock any barnacles off carefully with a knife.
3. Tumble the mussels into a saucepan and add the white wine. Clamp on the lid and cook for 3 minutes, until the mussels have opened fully.
4. Drain the mussels, reserving the cooking juices, and discard any mussels that have not opened fully.

5. Snap each shell and remove the mussels. Set them aside.
6. In a frying pan, heat the olive oil and fry the anchovies for a minute then add the garlic, chilli and capers. Mix well.
7. Chop up the mussels and add them to the frying pan with 3 tbsp reserved mussel juice.
8. Stir well, season with salt and pepper, then remove from the heat.
9. Add the breadcrumbs and lemon zest to the pan along with the chopped parsley and another small drizzle of olive oil.
10. Fill each mussel shell with the filling and lay them in an ovenproof dish. Bake for 10 minutes, until the breadcrumbs have become golden.
11. Drizzle with extra virgin olive oil to serve.

Fish Baked in Salt

Pesce al sale

Pesce al sale is such a simple way to cook fish, while holding in all the natural flavours and juices. This is one of the most popular ways fish is prepared in Italy, especially along the coast, where fresh fish is easily available. Puglia has the longest coastline of all the regions in Italy, so copious amounts of fresh fish feature in the Southern diet.

Preparation time: 15 minutes
Cooking time: 25 minutes
Serves: 2

2kg rock salt
4 egg whites
2 large fresh sea bass, gutted and cleaned, but with scales on
Small bunch thyme, chopped
Small bunch dill, chopped
4 garlic cloves, peeled and chopped
1 large lemon, sliced
1 large lemon, quartered into wedges to serve

1. Preheat the oven to 220°C (gas 7).
2. Combine the egg white and salt in a large bowl.
3. Spread a layer of the salt mixture on the base of a large baking tray.
4. Into the cavity of both fish tuck a combination of the dill, thyme, garlic and lemon slices.
5. Now place the filled fish on the baking tray. Squeeze over a spritz of lemon and pack the remaining salt on top of them. Ensure the complete fish is covered.
6. Bake in the oven for 25 minutes.

7. Once cooked, break through the salt crust with a wooden spoon then carefully remove the salt crust. Do this slowly so as not to damage the fish.
8. Removing the salt will normally take away the top layer of the skin. Lift off the top fillet, remove the inner bones and then take the second fillet out of the salt.
9. Serve with lemon wedges and a light salad or seasonal vegetables.

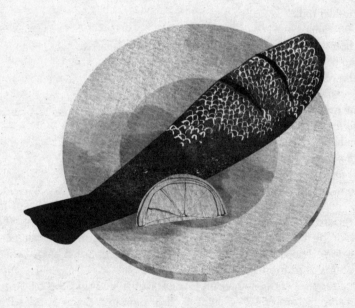

Fried Seafood

Fritto misto

Puglia is one of the less wealthy regions in Italy; however some say it's poor in money, but rich in flavour and food. With an abundance of fruit and vegetables, the breeze from the sea and the baking hot sun, there is no shortage of amazing local produce to accompany the freshest of fish and seafood. Fritto misto is the perfect dish to make the most of it all – you can use any fish or seafood, just try to include a good variety, with large wedges of bobbly Italian lemons.

Preparation time: 15 minutes
Cooking time: 20 minutes
Serves: 4

For the batter:
1 large egg
60ml full fat milk
120g '00' flour
60ml beer
Salt and pepper to season
500ml sunflower oil for deep frying
For the seafood and vegetables:
15 king prawns, cleaned and prepared
2 small squid, cleaned
250g mixed fish fillets, such as mullet and bass
2 small courgettes, sliced lengthways 10cm x 1cm
Fennel tops, to garnish
2 lemons, cut into wedges

1. Prepare the batter by beating the egg in a bowl with the milk. Add the flour, mix and pour in the beer. Season with salt and pepper. The batter should be thick in texture. Set it aside while you prepare the fish.
2. In a large shallow saucepan or deep fat fryer bring the oil up to a temperature of 170°C (test by dropping in a piece of bread, it should colour immediately).

3. Take the squid and cut it into 2cm pieces. Then cut the fish fillets into bite-sized chunks. Make sure that the prawns are cleaned and prepared.
4. Slice the courgettes into chunky batons or long wedges.
5. Once the oil is at the correct temperature, take a piece of fish, dip it in the batter and drop it into the oil; do this with no more than 5 pieces at a time. Use a slotted spoon to turn the fish. They should take approximately 5 minutes to cook.
6. Place the fried fish on some kitchen towel to drain off any excess oil, cover and place in a warm oven while you carry on cooking.
7. Repeat the process until all the fish, seafood and courgettes are cooked.
8. Serve on a large dish, garnished with chopped fennel tops and lemon wedges.

Linguine with Clams

Linguine con vongole

The Neapolitans have claimed this dish as their own, however each region of Italy adores this combination and each cooks it a little differently. Clams release an incredible sweetness to this dish and they marry up so well with the fresh leggy linguine. It takes just minutes to prepare and is wonderful to share.

Preparation time: 10 minutes
Cooking time: 12 minutes
Serves: 4

3 tbsp olive oil
2 garlic cloves, peeled and crushed
1 small chilli, halved and chopped, seeds removed
500g linguine
10 cherry tomatoes, halved
500g clams
150ml white wine
Salt and pepper to season
Small bunch parsley, chopped

1. Take a large saucepan, three quarters fill it with water and bring to a boil.
2. Wash the clams and ensure they are clean and that all individual clams are closed. Discard any that are not, as they will not be safe to eat.
3. Take a large frying pan and add 3 tbsp olive oil, bring to a gentle heat and add the garlic and chilli. Stir and cook for 1 minute.
4. Add the linguine to the pan of boiling water and cook according to the packet instructions.
5. Scatter the tomatoes into the frying pan and stir. Cook for 2 minutes.

6. Add the cleaned clams to the pan along with the white wine. Season with salt and pepper.
7. Scatter in half of the chopped parsley, stir and clamp on a lid. Shake the pan and cook for 3 minutes until the clams have all opened fully.
8. Once cooked, drain the linguine and add it to the clams. Stir to combine.
9. Serve on a large platter with the clams tumbled on top. Sprinkle over the remaining parsley.

Mussels with Tomatoes
Cozze con pomodoro

A steaming bowl of these irresistible mussels will tempt any seafood lover to the table; it's simple to prepare, light on the purse strings and a great dish to share. This dish would feed four as a starter or two as a main course, with fresh bread to dip into the silky sauce. Using fingers is an essential with this dish, so be prepared to get a little messy.

Preparation time: 10 minutes
Cooking time: 10 minutes
Serves: 4 (starter), 2 (main)

500g fresh mussels cleaned and prepared
2 tbsp olive oil
1 shallot, chopped
2 cloves garlic, crushed
1 glass white wine
400g tinned tomatoes
1 tbsp tomato purée
1 tsp thyme
1 tsp marjoram
1 small fresh chilli, chopped
Small bunch of parsley, chopped
Salt and pepper

1. Start by preparing the mussels. Pull off the loose beards and chip off any barnacles with a knife.
2. Place the mussels in a colander and wash well for 2 minutes under cold, running water to remove any grit and dirt. Shake well.
3. Discard any mussels that are already open.
4. Heat the olive oil in a large saucepan then tip in the chopped shallot and crushed garlic. Cook slowly for about 5 minutes until they are just soft.

5. Add the white wine and cook down for about 2 minutes.
6. Tumble in the tin of tomatoes, squeeze in the tomato purée, and add the dried herbs and lots of seasoning – salt, pepper, chilli and fresh herbs.
7. Cook for 5 minutes until the sauce has slightly thickened. Now add the cleaned mussels. Clamp on the lid and cook for around 3-4 minutes. Once the mussels have all opened, they are ready.
8. Finish with chopped parsley and shake the saucepan so that the mussels take on the tomato sauce.
9. Serve the mussels in a warm bowl with the sauce and a basket of fresh bread.

Carmela's tip

Mussels are in season through the months of September to April, so make the most of them when they are available. Remember, if the mussel is open already prior to cooking then it's no good. They should all be closed as they go into the pot and open when they have finished cooking. If any have not opened once cooked discard them.

Salt Cod with Tomatoes and Potatoes

Baccala con pomodoro e patate

This dish is another that symbolises Christmas to me, traditionally eaten on Christmas or New Year's Eve. Luckily for me, my good friend, Adriana Staniscia, runs the local Italian delicatessen known as The Italian Shop and throughout the month of December stocks baccala. A little bit of time and preparation is required prior to cooking this dish: the baccala must soak in cold water for at least three days and the water will require changing three times a day, but the preparation is essential and completely worthwhile.

Preparation time: 15 minutes
Cooking time: 1 hour 20 minutes
Serves: 4–6

125ml olive oil
1 white onion, finely sliced
2 garlic cloves, sliced
500g ripe tomatoes, peeled, seeds removed and chopped
400g tin chopped tomatoes
1kg salt cod (baccala), soaked as above
140g pitted olives
6 large potatoes, peeled and quartered
450ml water
Pepper to season (no salt)

1. Preheat the oven to 180°C (gas 4).
2. In a large, ovenproof casserole dish, heat the olive oil and fry off the onion and garlic until lightly softened.
3. Add the chopped fresh tomatoes along with the can of tomatoes, stir and cook for 20 minutes over a medium heat.
4. Add the baccala to the dish and tip in the olives and potatoes.
5. Pour in 450ml water and season with pepper. Cover and bake for 50 minutes, turning the salt cod half way through cooking.
6. Once cooked the baccala should easily flake away from the bone. Serve on a large platter with rustic bread.

Vegetables, Sides and Salads

Roasted peppers, fried courgette flowers filled with ricotta cheese or fennel and Parmesan salad anyone? Always use fruit and vegetables when they are in season, as this is when they are at their cheapest as well as their best – even better, buy extra when you can and preserve or prepare food for the freezer for when produce is out of season. The recipes in this section can be served as a light lunch or starter or alongside a main course as an accompaniment. There are no rules, but I have made suggestions for what you might serve these dishes with.

Bread Salad
Panzanella

A fresh and simple recipe from the beautiful region of Tuscany, La Toscana. In most bread bins you will find a small piece of stale and forgotten bread, but this is its chance to shine. The bread absorbs all the dressing and the flavour of the tomatoes in a way that fresh bread would not. If you prepare this salad in advance, it will improve with time as the flavours will have a chance to mellow together.

Preparation time: 10 minutes
Serves: 4

400g day-old rustic bread
2 tbsp water
1 small red onion, peeled and sliced
6 ripe vine tomatoes, chopped
Small cucumber, chopped into small chunks
Large bunch of basil, torn
Salt and pepper to season
6 tbsp extra virgin olive oil
2 tbsp white wine vinegar

1. Roughly cube the bread and place it in a bowl.
2. Sprinkle over the water to soften the bread.
3. Slice the onion, chop the tomatoes and cucumber and tumble into the bread, then stir well.
4. Scatter the torn basil over the salad and season with salt and pepper to taste.
5. Drizzle over the extra virgin olive oil and vinegar and mix well.
6. Serve either as a starter or as an accompanying dish.

Fennel and Parmesan Salad
Finnochio con parmigiano

Fennel has an aniseed hit, yet is very refreshing on the palate. At Christmas time I normally buy a box of fennel bulbs from our local Italian delicatessen, clean and quarter them, then immerse them in cold water and place in the fridge for the festive season. Finely sliced, perhaps tossed with a few green salad leaves, they will freshen your palate after a heavy meal and help with digestion.

Preparation time: 10 minutes
Serves: 4

3 fennel bulbs, halved and sliced
90g Parmesan
3 tbsp olive oil
Salt and pepper

1. Wash, halve and finely slice the fennel bulbs. Lay the fennel on a flat plate.
2. Using a vegetable peeler, slice the Parmesan so you have fine long slices or shards and drape them over the prepared fennel.
3. Drizzle over the olive oil and add a generous grind of salt and pepper.
4. Serve immediately alongside grilled fish, lamb or pork.

Filled Baby Peppers
Peperoni ripiene

These peperoni are just delicious – sweet and rich in colour, delicate in shape, yet a little plump in figure. When the peppers have been roasted, the sweetness is incredible and the filling becomes moist with a little crunch on top. Try to be careful and keep the stalks on when you slice the peppers lengthways – not only for colour and appearance but because they help to hold the whole peperoni together when full.

Preparation time: 15 minutes
Cooking time: 25 minutes
Serves: 4

10 small peppers, halved
100g fresh breadcrumbs
50g Parmesan, grated
1 tsp bicarbonate of soda
2 cloves garlic, crushed
Small sprig oregano and thyme, chopped
Small bunch basil, chopped
Salt and pepper to season
A little pinch of chilli or a small fresh chilli
2 eggs

1. Preheat the oven to 190°C (gas 5).
2. Slice the peppers lengthways, carefully cutting through the stem, so that some remains attached to each half. Remove the white internal pith and seeds. Place into a baking dish.
3. Put the breadcrumbs, Parmesan, bicarbonate of soda, garlic, herbs, salt, pepper, chilli and eggs all in a bowl. Mix the ingredients well together.

4. Fill the peppers with the breadcrumb mixture using a teaspoon, making sure they are full to the brim. A tight fit in the dish will help to keep them in shape.
5. Drizzle over a little olive oil and sprinkle with fresh thyme. Bake for 25 minutes.

Carmela's tip

If you double the amount of filling above you can make extra. The peppers keep in the fridge for three days and are ideal as an antipasti dish, side dish, squashed between some bread or as an accompaniment to a main meal.

Filled Romano Peppers

Peperoni romano riempire

Peppers that have been roasted in the oven have an irresistible sweetness. They are delicious simply baked in some olive oil, garlic and fresh herbs, but filled with a delicious fresh filling they become a meal.

Preparation time: 15 minutes
Cooking time: 25 minutes
Serves: 4

4 romano peppers
12 cherry tomatoes, quartered
200g fresh breadcrumbs
30g pecorino, grated
2 large cloves garlic, sliced
20 green olives, sliced
Large handful of fresh basil, chopped
1 tbsp capers, finely chopped
Salt and pepper to season
250g mozzarella, sliced and cubed
Extra virgin olive oil to drizzle

1. Preheat the oven to 190°C (gas 5).
2. Slice the peppers lengthways and place on a baking tray lined with tin foil. Try to keep the green stalks on as they hold the pepper intact and also look lovely.
3. Drizzle a little olive oil over the peppers, then fill them evenly with the quartered cherry tomatoes.
4. Put the breadcrumbs in a bowl together with the pecorino, garlic, olives, basil, capers, and salt and pepper. Mix well.

5. Now fill each of the peppers with the breadcrumb mixture and press the filling down. Sprinkle chopped mozzarella over each pepper, drizzle with olive oil and bake until the cheese has melted.
6. Serve as a starter or alongside meat, poultry or fish.

Filled Courgette Flowers
Fiori di zucca ripieni

Courgette flowers are delicate and delicious stuffed and filled with herbs and cheese, then dipped into a light batter and fried. The smaller the courgette flower the better the taste. Female flowers are attached to a small courgette while the male flowers just have a stalk. Both flowers are edible, so snap them up if you find them in the greengrocer's or if you grow them in your own garden.

Preparation time: 15 minutes
Cooking time: 10 minutes
Serves: 6

12 courgette flowers
300g fresh ricotta cheese
50g Parmesan, grated
4 anchovies, chopped
Pinch of nutmeg
Zest of a small lemon
Pepper to season
For the batter:
200g plain flour
1 tsp bicarbonate of soda
Pinch of salt
250ml water
6 tbsp sunflower oil

1. Prepare the courgette flowers, brush away any dirt and remove the long centre pistils in the middle. Set to one side.
2. Prepare the filling by placing the ricotta in a bowl and breaking it down with a fork.
3. Add the grated Parmesan, chopped anchovies, nutmeg and lemon zest. Stir well and season with pepper.
4. Prepare the batter by adding the flour, bicarbonate of soda, salt and water to a bowl. Using a hand whisk, incorporate well until you have a light batter. If time allows let the batter rest in the fridge for 30 minutes, but this stage is not essential.

5. Fill each flower head with the cheese filling.
6. When all the flower heads are ready add the sunflower oil to a frying pan and heat. Dip each flower into the batter and shallow fry on each side until golden.
7. Drain the fried flowers on kitchen roll to absorb any excess fat.
8. Serve immediately with a light salad.

Frittata with Courgette and Potato

Frittata con zucchini e patate

As a mother, it is essential to be able to magically come up with something delicious, healthy and filling to eat. I think it may be in an Italian mother's contract. This is one of my children's favourite meals, and thankfully it's simple too: dinner is on the table within 15 minutes from start to finish. The great benefit of a frittata is that you can make it very simple, or hot and spicy and deep with filling, depending on what you have available. Our favourite combination is potato, onion and courgette, but you can vary this with fresh seasonal asparagus, peppers and greens. Frittata is delicious hot or cold, so keep any leftovers for sandwiches.

Preparation time: 5 minutes
Cooking time: 15 minutes
Serves: 6

5 tbsp olive oil
1 red onion, peeled and chopped
2 small potatoes, peeled and cubed
1 medium courgette, sliced
8 eggs
60g Parmesan, grated
1 small bunch basil, torn
Salt and pepper to season

1. In a frying pan, heat about 3 tbsp olive oil and fry the onion and potato on a medium heat until cooked through and slightly golden; this will take around 10 minutes. Then add the sliced discs of courgette and fry for a further 2 minutes.
2. Crack all the eggs into a bowl and whisk. Add the Parmesan, torn up basil and a little salt and pepper.
3. Now add the remaining olive oil to the frying pan, turn up the heat and tip in the egg mixture. With a spatula push the mixture down and allow it to cook on one side.
4. To cook the other side, place a plate on top of the frittata and flip it over to turn it out.
5. Now slide the frittata back into the frying pan and cook on the reverse side for a further 3 minutes.
6. Serve as an addition to antipasti, as a simple lunch or alongside a main meal.

Green Bean Salad

Insalata di fagioline

This salad can be served warm or cold. It is a favourite vegetable snack to have in the fridge in our house and also goes well alongside most main meat or fish dishes. It can be ready within five minutes and is especially wonderful in the height of summer, when there are many deliciously sweet, seasonal green beans available.

Preparation time: 3 minutes
Cooking time: 5–7 minutes
Serves: 6

600g green beans
2 cloves garlic, finely sliced
2 tbsp parsley, chopped
1 tbsp basil, chopped
2 tbsp red wine vinegar
6 tbsp extra virgin olive oil

1. Top and tail the green beans.
2. Take a saucepan and three quarters fill it with water. Bring the water to boil and add a good pinch of salt.
3. Add the beans to the water and cook for around 5 minutes, until they are tender but still al dente.
4. Take the beans off the heat and drain then plunge them into a bowl of ice cold water. This will stop them from cooking any further and will hold the vibrant green colour. Leave them in the water for 5 minutes.
5. Drain the beans and dry them with kitchen towel. Place into a large serving dish.
6. Scatter over the finely sliced garlic, chopped parsley and basil.
7. Pour over the vinegar and stir then drizzle over the oil. Stir again and season with salt and pepper.
8. Serve alongside grilled fish or meat.

Carmela's tip

Buy green beans in bulk when they are in season, blanch quickly in boiling water, cool and then freeze for use when you cannot buy fresh.

Marrow Parmigiana with Italian Sausage Sauce
Parmigiana con zuccona

Through the summer I have access to marrows in abundance. They are, in essence, overgrown zucchini, and I'm sure my parents are unable to spot them beneath the leaves until it's too late and they have grown huge. In our house we know marrow as *cogotzze*, a giant oversized monster of a courgette. Perfect for a full family get together, this hot parmigiana in the centre of the table with a leafy salad and large basket of bread is my idea of perfection.

Preparation time: sugo, 10 minutes, fritters, 20 minutes; parmigiana, 10 minutes
Cooking time: sugo, 1 hour 30 minutes, parmigiana 1 hour 10 minutes
Serves: 8

For the sauce:
2 tbsp olive oil
290g Italian hard sausage
1 clove garlic, peeled and crushed
700g passata
250ml water
Salt and pepper
2 tbsp tomato purée
1 bay leaf
Small handful basil, chopped
For the marrow:
2 medium marrows, cut into disks
350g plain flour
1 tsp salt
Pepper to season
3 eggs
300ml milk
Sunflower oil to fry
500g mozzarella, chopped
30g Parmesan

1. Preheat the oven to 180° C (gas 4).
2. Cut the sausage into bite-sized pieces and place in a medium saucepan with the olive oil.
3. Fry the sausage until coloured, then add the garlic and stir. Cook for a further minute.
4. Pour in the passata and water. Stir well and season with salt, pepper, tomato purée, bay leaf and the chopped basil. Cook on a medium heat for 1 hour 30 minutes.
5. To prepare the batter, add the flour, salt, pepper, eggs and milk to a large bowl and stir using a whisk. Place the batter in the fridge to chill for 30 minutes.
6. Cut the marrows into slices. Take a large frying pan and warm 4 tbsp of oil over a medium heat.
7. Dip each marrow disk into the batter and fry in the oil until golden in colour. They should take a minute or so on each side. Drain on kitchen towel and repeat with the other marrow disks.
8. To assemble the parmigiana. Take an ovenproof dish, 25cm x 30cm, and add a ladle of the sugo to cover the base in a thin layer of sauce.
9. Take each marrow disk, dip lightly into the sauce and place in the dish. Create a layer of marrow followed by a sprinkling of mozzarella and then a ladle of sugo. Then repeat the process again.
10. Aim for three layers and finish off with mozzarella on the top. Sprinkle over some Parmesan and cover with foil.
11. Bake for 1 hour then remove the foil and cook for a further 10 minutes.
12. Serve with a fresh leafy salad.

Mozzarella Sandwich

Mozzarella in carrozza

Mozzarella is a fresh cheese, originally from southern Italy, traditionally made from Italian buffalo and later cows' milk. Mozzarella is a staple ingredient and one that can always be found in my fridge, as it is useful in so many dishes, from the topping of a pizza to layered between a lasagne or pasta dish. Snack time means only one thing in my house, mozzarella in carrozza.

Preparation time: 10 minutes
Cooking time: 5 minutes
Serves: 4

8 slices white bread
300g mozzarella, sliced
150ml milk
5 tbsp plain flour
2 large eggs, beaten
Salt and pepper to season
4 tbsp olive oil to fry

1. Cut the crusts off the white bread. Make four mozzarella sandwiches, leaving the edges unfilled with cheese.
2. Press the sandwiches all the way around the outside using the tips of your fingers. This will seal them so you have no mozzarella escaping.
3. You will need to use three separate bowls: one for the milk, one for the flour and one for the beaten eggs. Season the eggs with a little salt and pepper.
4. Dip each sealed sandwich into the milk then the flour and the egg.
5. Fry each sandwich separately in a little olive oil until golden in colour on both sides, and place on some kitchen towel to dry up any excess oil. Keep each sandwich warm until all four are cooked.

Carmela's tip

This is great Italian fast food on the go! Eat immediately, but with caution as the filling will be piping hot.

Rice Salad

Insalata di riso

Rice is a staple ingredient in Northern Italy, where it grows in abundance in the regions of Lombardy and Piedmont, however every Southern Italian home will have a bag of rice in their store cupboard. This salad is one that I make for a family gathering; it keeps very well in the fridge (in a sealed container) and will accompany fish and meat beautifully. You can alter the recipe by using what vegetables you have in your fridge.

Preparation time: 15 minutes
Cooking time: 12 minutes
Serves: 4–6

500g long grain rice
4 vine tomatoes, chopped
¼ cucumber, diced
1 stalk celery, finely chopped
30g green olives, pitted and halved
1 small red onion, finely chopped
2 spring onions, sliced
1 bell pepper, cubed
Small bunch basil, chopped
4 tbsp olive oil
Salt and pepper to season

1. Cook the rice in salted water according to the packet instructions, until tender.
2. Take a large bowl and add the tomatoes, cucumber, celery, olives, red onion, spring onion and pepper. Stir well.
3. Drain the rice and allow it to cool thoroughly.
4. Once cool tumble the rice into the prepared chopped vegetables and stir through thoroughly. Scatter in the chopped basil.
5. Dress with olive oil and season with salt and pepper. Taste and check for seasoning.
6. Serve with fish or meat or as part of a picnic.

Filled Romano Peppers with Lentils

Peperoni con lenticchie

I think that I may have a small obsession with stuffing peppers. I adore frying peppers in olive oil with a little garlic and running them through pasta, but roasted in the oven they are amazing and so intensely sweet. Romano peppers are a complete meal in themselves, particularly when stuffed with lentils, and these require no other accompaniment – they are filling, fresh, full of flavour and fabulous.

Preparation time: 10 minutes
Cooking time: 25 minutes
Serves: 2–4

2 romano peppers
560ml vegetable stock
80g lentils
125g mozzarella, cubed
10 olives, sliced
Large handful basil, torn
Oregano, a few fresh leaves
Salt and pepper to season
Olive oil to drizzle

1. Preheat the oven to 190°C (gas 5).
2. Slice the peppers lengthways, cutting through the green stalk whilst being careful to keep it attached. Place the peppers on a baking tray.
3. Add the vegetables and lentils to a saucepan and cook according to the packet instructions for the lentils. Ensure that the lentils retain a slight bite, then strain and season with a little salt and pepper.
4. Mix the mozzarella, olives, basil and oregano leaves in a bowl.
5. Fill the peppers with the lentil and vegetable stuffing, then top with generous amounts of the mozzarella mixture.
6. Drizzle with olive oil and bake in the oven for around 25 minutes.
7. Serve with a leafy salad.

Seasonal Spinach with Crushed Tomatoes

Spinaci al pomodoro

Tomatoes are the sweetest of fruits and an incredible range is available, from plump, fresh tomatoes grown in the hot Mediterranean sun to full preserved tomatoes and passata sauces. Tomatoes are an absolute essential to any Italian garden and kitchen and this recipe showcases *cucina povera* cooking at its best. This dish would accompany any main course, but is just as perfect scooped up – warm – from a bowl with a piece of torn-off bread and a glass of vino rosso.

Preparation time: 5 minutes
Cooking time: 20 minutes
Serves: 4

4 tbsp olive oil
2 cloves garlic, finely sliced
300g spinach
1 x 400g tin plum tomatoes
Small handful basil, chopped
Salt and pepper
½ tsp chilli flakes

1. Add the oil to a medium saucepan and gently fry the garlic for 5 minutes.
2. Wash the spinach and wilt it in a dry frying pan on a low heat for 3 minutes. Drain into a colander and squeeze between your hands to remove any excess water.
3. Add the tomatoes to the saucepan with the garlic and stir. Using the back of a fork gently squeeze the tomatoes.
4. Add the drained spinach and stir, then season with chopped basil, salt, pepper and a little chilli. Cook on a medium heat for a further 15 minutes.
5. Serve in warm bowls as a side dish or with rustic bread.

Simple Beans

Fagioli a soluti

This one-bowl dish is one of my mother Solidea's favourite recipes, and typifies the traditional *cucina povera* style of cooking. This recipe uses tins from the store cupboard plus a few fresh flavours to produce a bowl of mellow golden beans.

Preparation times: 5 minutes
Cooking time: 10 minutes
Serves: 2–4

400g can cannellini beans
400g can chickpeas
A bean can full of water
1 clove garlic, crushed
1 chicken stock cube
3 tbsp olive oil
Leaves from 3 celery stalks, chopped finely
Salt and pepper to season

1. Pour the cannellini beans and chickpeas into a saucepan.
2. Fill one of the tins with water and pour into the pan with the beans and stir.
3. Add the crushed garlic, stock cube, olive oil, chopped celery leaves and stir.
4. Squash and break down the beans.
5. Simmer for 15 minutes and season with salt and pepper to taste.
6. Serve with Italian bread to dip into the beans and to scrape up every last morsel from the bowl. It is delicious any time of the day.

Simple Potato Salad

Insalata di patate

Small potatoes with their jackets left on, dressed with extra virgin olive oil, garlic and chopped parsley: it is the simple foods and flavours that we love to eat at our family table. Here the potatoes are served cold and would accompany chicken, pork cotollette or grilled fish with a light salad.

Preparation time: 5 minutes
Cooking time: 15 minutes
Serves: 6–8

700g new potatoes
3 cloves garlic, finely sliced
2 tbsp parsley, chopped
6 tbsp extra virgin olive oil
Salt and pepper, to season
1 small red chilli, finely sliced

1. Halve the new potatoes and boil in salted water until tender.
2. Once the potatoes are cool, tumble them into a large bowl and dress them with sliced garlic.
3. Scatter over the chopped parsley and drizzle over the extra virgin olive oil.
4. Stir well and season with salt and pepper; a little chilli could be added for a gentle heat.
5. Serve with fish or meat and a salad.

Italian Roasted Potatoes with Garlic and Rosemary

Patate con aglio e rosmarino

Roasted with herbs, this is one of my favourite ways to prepare and cook potatoes. The flavour of the freshly roasted garlic and verdant rosemary is moreish and in my opinion beats normal roasted potatoes hands down.

Preparation time: 15 minutes
Cooking time: 1 hour
Serves: 6–8

2kg maris piper potatoes, peeled and sliced into wedges
2 large sprigs fresh rosemary, roughly chopped
4 cloves garlic, halved
5–6 tbsp olive oil
Salt and pepper to season

1. Preheat the oven to 200°C (gas 6).
2. Place the quartered potato wedges onto a large baking tray.
3. Sprinkle over the rosemary and garlic, drizzle with olive oil and season with salt and pepper.
4. Shake the tray to ensure all the potatoes are coated in olive oil.
5. Bake in the oven until golden.
6. Serve alongside any fish or meat.

Carmela's tip
A great alternative would be to use sweet potatoes.

Slow Stewed Peppers

Peperonata

If you love slow cooked peppers then this dish of peperonata will become a regular dish on your family menu. It makes a great accompaniment to fish or meat, or piled on some freshly toasted bread. I also run pasta through the peperonata if I am looking for more of a substantial low cost meal. Any excuse to use pasta, I will find it! Cooking peppers really brings out the sweet flavour in them and this recipe is one that is not only simple but only uses ingredients that you are likely to have already in your store cupboard or fridge.

Preparation time: 10 minutes
Cooking time: 1 hour
Serves: 4

4 tbsp olive oil
4 large bell peppers, cut into bite-sized chunks
3 cloves garlic, sliced
2 red onions, sliced
100ml red wine
200ml passata
1 sprig fresh marjoram leaves (or oregano)
Salt and pepper to season
Small bunch basil, chopped

1. Pour the olive oil into a sauté pan and bring to a gentle heat. Tumble in the prepared peppers and cook gently for 15 minutes.
2. Add the sliced garlic along with the sliced red onion and slowly fry off with the peppers. Cook for about 10 minutes.
3. Pour in the red wine, reduce and cook down for 5 minutes and then pour in the passata, sprinkle in the marjoram and season with salt and pepper. Cover and cook for 30 minutes on a medium heat. Stir occasionally.
4. Serve with pasta or spooned alongside grilled fish or meat.

Solidea's Parmigiana

Parmigiana di melanzane

Here is one of our favourite family recipes, straight from my mother Solidea's kitchen. From my childhood I remember the sliced bright purple aubergines sitting in a colander over the kitchen sink, sprinkled with salt. In Puglia when they make parmigiana, the aubergine is pan fried in a light batter, whereas in other regions the aubergine will be coated and fried in breadcrumbs or even just flour.

Preparation time: 30 minutes, not including salting
Cooking time: 1 hour
Serves: 6

500ml tomato sauce (sugo) (page 38)
4 small aubergines, sliced lengthways
A handful of salt
260g plain flour
1 large egg, whisked
1 pint milk
Salt and pepper to season
800g mozzarella, chopped

1. Slice the aubergines lengthways into thin slices, place in a colander and sprinkle liberally with salt. The reason for doing this is to draw out the moisture from the aubergines. The aubergines need to sit in the colander for a minimum of 2 hours to as long as 24 hours.
2. When the aubergines are ready, give each slice a squeeze to remove any excess water and wipe dry using a kitchen towel to remove any excess salt. Place them onto a piece of kitchen towel; they will be a little floppy and discoloured.
3. Preheat the oven to 190°C (gas 5) while you prepare the batter.
4. Into a bowl, pour the flour, egg and milk. Give it a really good whisk, season with salt and pepper and leave to one side.

5. In a frying pan add a glug of olive oil. Dip each aubergine slice into the batter and fry until lightly golden on each side. Then place on a plate with kitchen towel to absorb any excess oil whilst you fry the remaining aubergines.

6. Spoon a ladle of your sugo into an ovenproof dish, so that it just coats the base. Lay the aubergines in a single layer on top of the sugo and sprinkle over a little mozzarella, then add another ladle of sugo. Repeat the layers until you have four layers.

7. The last layer should end with mozzarella and sugo, then scatter some freshly torn basil on top.

8. Cover the parmigiana with foil and bake for 30 minutes then remove the foil for the last 30 minutes to allow the parmigiana to turn golden and slightly crispy around the edges.

9. Allow the parmigiana to stand for 10 minutes before slicing.

10. Serve with salad and sliced bread.

Carmela's tip

I still salt the aubergines, although many cooks nowadays think this is not necessary. Try it both ways and decide for yourself.

Spring Dandelion Greens with Chilli and Garlic

Cicoria con aglio e peperoncino

I take my basket and go foraging for dandelion leaves in our local forest any time from the end of March to mid-May. They can be found everywhere and cost absolutely nothing. Make sure that you pick lots as they wilt down considerably once cooked. Eaten raw, the leaves have a bitter taste to them, but once cooked they seem to release a little sweetness. Kale or cavolo nero would also work really well.

Preparation time: 3 minutes
Cooking time: 8 minutes
Serves: 4

600g dandelion leaves
4 tbsp olive oil
2 cloves garlic, sliced
Pinch chilli flakes
Salt and pepper to season

1. Wash the dandelion leaves thoroughly to ensure you have removed any dirt and grit.
2. Take a large saucepan of water and bring it to a rapid boil. Add a large pinch of salt.
3. Drop in the dandelion leaves and blanch for 3 minutes, drain and set aside.
4. In a frying pan, heat the olive oil over a medium heat. Add the garlic, stir and cook gently for 3 minutes.
5. Add the dandelion leaves to the garlic, sprinkle over the chilli and cook for a further 5 minutes.
6. Serve alongside fish or meat, or over some toasted bread.

Courgette Fritters
Zucchine fritte

Courgettes are a summery treat. They are one of the easiest vegetables to grow – one plant will produce an astonishing yield – and they are super-quick to prepare and cook. In Italy courgettes are one of the most popular vegetables after the voluptuous, ruby red tomato of course. Coarsely grated and fried, stuffed, chopped into a frittata, and cooked through pasta as well as ribboned through a salad: the cooking varieties are endless.

Preparation time: 15 minutes
Cooking time: 15 minutes
Serves: 4

4 medium courgettes, grated
1 large onion, grated
1 small bunch parsley, chopped
1 small bunch basil, chopped
1 small chilli, finely chopped
1 tsp dried oregano
Salt and pepper to season
2 eggs, beaten
6 tbsp plain flour
150ml sunflower oil, for frying

1. Mix together the courgettes and onion then add the parsley and basil, and mix again.
2. Into the bowl add the finely chopped chilli, dried oregano and salt and pepper. Give it all a good stir.
3. Crack in the eggs and sprinkle in the flour. With a spatula incorporate the eggs and flour well with the vegetables and herbs. You are looking for a dropping consistency.
4. Add the sunflower oil to a frying pan and spoon in four heaped tablespoons of the mixture, in separate blobs.
5. Cook until golden brown on one side and flip on to the other side for a further 2 minutes so they are beautifully golden on each side.
6. Place each fritter onto a piece of kitchen towel to soak up any excess grease. Repeat until you have used all the mixture.
7. Serve as a starter or alongside a main meal. However, my favourite serving suggestion would be to have the fried courgette squashed in between two thick slices of rustic bread.

Stuffed Aubergines

Melanzane ripiene

Plump and delicious, these stuffed aubergines are a substantial dish and score highly as a family favourite in our house. Aubergines are like sponges and are full of moisture, so I salt mine overnight to draw it out, but once that is done, this recipe is easy and quick to prepare and just requires a slow bake.

Preparation time: 20 minutes
Cooking time: 1 hour 30 minutes
Serves: 4–6

3 medium aubergines
4 tbsp olive oil and a little to drizzle
200g pancetta, chopped
125g mushrooms, peeled and finely chopped
2 garlic cloves, crushed
200g fresh breadcrumbs
200g Edam cheese, grated
½ tsp chilli flakes
Handful basil, chopped
350g passata
Salt and pepper to season

1. Preheat the oven to 160°C (gas 3).
2. Cut each aubergine in half lengthways. Score the inner pulp with a knife and scoop out the cubed flesh. This should leave you with an empty boat ready to be filled.
3. Fry the pancetta in the olive oil until browned and cook for 5 minutes.
4. Add the aubergine pulp, chopped mushrooms and garlic. Stir and cook until the aubergine has softened, about 5–10 minutes.
5. Remove the mixture from the heat and scatter over the breadcrumbs, cheese, chilli and basil.

6. Ladle over half the passata sauce, season with salt and pepper and stir well to combine.
7. Take each aubergine boat and spoon in the prepared mixture. Place the aubergines into an ovenproof dish.
8. Spoon over the remaining passata and drizzle over a little olive oil. Cover with foil and bake for 60 minutes until the aubergines are tender. Remove the foil and continue to cook for a further 30 minutes to allow the parmigiana to brown.
9. Serve with a salad.

Carmela's tip
You can also make this recipe with courgettes.

Spinach Pesto
Spinaci pesto

Everyone loves pesto, whether it's simply spooned through trofie pasta, stirred into a risotto, seductively drizzled over a tomato and fresh burrata salad starter or used as a topping on toasted bread, the uses are truly endless. This spinach pesto is a favourite of mine. I normally make a medium-sized jar of this verdant paste and top it up with olive oil before placing in the fridge, where it will keep for up to a month.

Preparation time: 5 minutes
Makes: 500ml jar

200g freshly washed and dried spinach
60g pine nuts untoasted
1 large clove garlic
60g parmesan
Twist of ground salt and pepper
80ml olive oil

1. Place the spinach, pine nuts, peeled garlic, Parmesan, salt and pepper into a food processor and blitz for 30 seconds.
2. Pour in half of the oil and blitz for a further 30 seconds. Slowly pour in the remaining oil until you have achieved the perfect pesto, a loose dropping consistency would be ideal.
3. Spoon into a sterilised jar and top with a little olive oil.

Pasta and Gnocchi

I just could not imagine life without pasta.

Whether it's a simple lunch dish or a larger, slightly greedier bowl for dinner, it's far healthier than rice and is incredibly versatile to use. You can pair pasta with a tomato sauce, a pesto paste or olive oil then add vegetables and seafood for a delectable and filling dish.

In Italy, there are around 600 pasta shapes available, giving ample choice for every sauce and palate. Whichever you choose, pasta needs to be cooked in a large saucepan with plenty of water. It's a good idea to work on the basis of 1 litre of water to every 100g of pasta. Also always remember to salt the water well. Italians say that 'the water should be as salty as the Mediterranean sea', approximately 1 teaspoon of salt to every 1 litre of water.

Gnocchi are also known as potato dumplings, but they are far lighter than that name suggests and are very simple to make. As a child, gnocchi were something I would turn my nose up at because I found them to be heavy and a little cloggy in my mouth, however making your own takes half an hour and they taste just scrumptious, delicate and very light.

Simple Egg Pasta Dough

Pasta fresca fatto a mano

So many people are afraid of making fresh handmade pasta, but why? I agree that ready-made dried pasta is affordable and a great staple store cupboard ingredient, however a bowl of freshly handmade pasta is simply mouth-watering from the first to the last bite. In my opinion, fresh pasta is superior to dried pasta not only in taste but in texture and colour also. When making fresh egg pasta '00' flour is used; the flour has been milled to a super fine powder and is much finer than other flours. '00' flour is also very good for baking with as it produces a lighter cake.

Preparation time: 1 hour (including resting time)
Serves: 4

400g '00' flour
4 large eggs
Pinch of salt

1. Ideally use a wooden or marble board. I prefer to use a wooden board as this gives a little added texture to the dough and helps in the kneading process. Pour the flour onto the board and form a well in the centre, I call this a volcano.
2. Crack the eggs into the well (volcano) and add a pinch of salt. Alternatively, crack the eggs into a bowl and whisk, add the salt and then tip into the well.
3. With your fingertips or a fork gradually incorporate the flour into the egg mixture, increasing the amount of flour as you go along.
4. Form the mixture into dough.
5. Knead the dough until it has become smooth and silky with a light spring back when pushed with your fingertip. Kneading by hand may take 7-10 minutes.
6. If the dough is a little dry add 1-2 tbsp water, if the dough is too wet add a little more flour.
7. Wrap the dough with cling film and allow to rest for a minimum of 30 minutes in the fridge.

8. Once the dough has rested you can either work and roll the dough by hand using a very thin rolling pin (I use a broom handle), or alternatively use a pasta machine. By using a pasta machine this allows the dough to become silky and guarantees a smooth finish.

9. Cut the dough in half. Take the first half and wrap the remaining with cling film. This will ensure the dough does not dry out and form an outer skin.

10. Set the pasta machine to the widest setting. Each machine will differ so please follow instructions as required.

11. Flatten and lightly flour the dough and feed through the pasta machine. Fold the dough back over itself and feed through the widest setting at least 6 times. This will ensure smoothness and elasticity to the dough.

12. Increase a notch on the machine and feed the dough through on each setting twice. There is no need to keep refolding the dough at this stage; you are just trying to lengthen the dough.

13. Continue rolling the dough, narrowing the rollers at every stage.

14. I tend to stop at the second-to-last thinnest section on the pasta machine. This is the appropriate thickness required for perfect pasta.

15. Now choose your shape, from spaghetti, linguine, lasagne sheets, tagliatelle or a perfect base for a filled ravioli, mezzaluna or tortellini.

Baked Rigatoni

Pasta sotto forno

A delicious, simple and very quick meal to prepare, particularly if you have a batch of bolognese sauce left over from making tagliatelle. You can also use a simple sauce like the pizza sauce (page 35), just double the quantity. Rigatoni is an ideal pasta for baking, as it is robust. The mozzarella adds moisture to the bake, so leftovers are perfect warmed up the following day too.

Preparation time: 15 minutes
Cooking time: 1 hour
Serves: 6

500g rigatoni
Bolognese sugo (page 26)
500g mozzarella, cubed
70g Parmesan, grated
20 basil leaves

1. Preheat the oven to 180°C (gas 4).
2. Cook the pasta in salted water, but drain it 4 minutes before it is al dente.
3. Mix two ladles of the bolognese sugo through the pasta to coat and colour it.
4. Take a large ovenproof dish and ladle over a thin layer of sugo to cover the base.
5. Add a layer of rigatoni and sprinkle over a layer of mozzarella cubes, a few basil leaves and 2 tbsp Parmesan.
6. Spoon over another ladle of sauce and repeat the layers.
7. Finish off with mozzarella cubes, Parmesan and a drizzle of the sauce.
8. Cover the dish with foil and bake for 40 minutes. Remove the foil and place back into the oven for a further 20 minutes until slightly golden.

Bucatini with Anchovies and Capers

Bucatini alla puttanesca

Puttanesca, in my opinion, sounds delicious as it rolls off the tongue, but the story behind the meaning is rather interesting. This recipe is what ladies of the night in Naples would make for their dinner after a busy evening on the town. So clearly this dish would need to be quick to prepare in order to satisfy a raging hunger deep into the night.

Preparation time: 5 minutes
Cooking time: 10 minutes
Serves: 4

500g bucatini
5 tbsp olive oil
1 garlic clove, peeled and sliced
1 small chilli, seeds removed and finely chopped
7 anchovy fillets, drained and chopped
50g salted capers, rinsed
100g pitted olives, halved
2 x 400g tins chopped tomatoes
Salt to season

1. Place a large pan of water on to boil, salting the water well.
2. Heat the oil in a large frying pan and add the garlic, chilli and anchovies. Cook for 2 minutes.
3. Once the water is bubbling add the bucatini and cook according to the packet instructions, less 1 minute.
4. Add the capers and olives to the frying pan, stir well and add the tinned tomatoes.
5. Season with a pinch of salt and cook for 10 minutes.
6. Drain the pasta and stir through the sauce. Serve immediately in warm bowls.

Cannelloni

Cannelloni di formaggio

Cannelloni are filled sheets of fresh pasta rolled and baked in the oven until golden and bubbling. The fillings can vary from simple light spinach and ricotta to meat-based fillings and vegetable offerings, such as artichoke and radicchio. Baked pasta is traditional on a Sunday lunch table, whether it be cannelloni, lasagne or conchiglioni – filled pasta shells.

Preparation time: 25 minutes
Cooking time: 50 minutes
Serves: 4

250g mozzarella, chopped finely
350g ricotta
130g pecorino, grated
10 button mushrooms, sliced
1 egg
2 tbsp parlsey, chopped
1 tbsp basil, chopped
Salt and pepper to season
300g fresh lasagne sheets
700g ready-made sugo (page 38)

1. Preheat the oven to 180°C (gas 4).
2. First, make the filling. Take a large bowl and add the mozzarella, ricotta, 60g of pecorino, mushrooms, egg, herbs and season with salt and pepper.
3. Mix with a fork until all the ingredients are well incorporated. Add 4 tbsp of the ready-made sugo and stir.
4. Take the lasagne sheets and cut them in half along the long edge. Put 4 tsp filling down the centre of each piece and roll them up into cannelloni.

5. Spoon a ladle of the sauce in the bottom of an ovenproof dish then lay the cannelloni on top. If they are a tight fit in the dish, they will be less likely to unroll as they cook.

6. Spoon over the remaining tomato sauce and sprinkle over the remaining pecorino.

7. Bake in the centre of the oven for 50 minutes, until the cheese has melted and is golden in colour.

8. Before serving, allow the cannelloni to stand for 10 minutes.

9. Serve with a leafy seasonal salad.

Linguine with Squid
Linguine con calamari

Traditionally served on Christmas Eve, but equally good on any day of the year, this sauce showcases Italian cooking and simplicity at its best. Calamari either needs to be cooked very quickly or simmered slowly to avoid it becoming tough and chewy. For me, this dish evokes memories of the night before Christmas when the smell would permeate through the house and the excitement of Christmas would begin.

Preparation time: 10 minutes
Cooking time: 1 hour 25 minutes
Serves: 4

250g cleaned calamari
2 tbsps olive oil
2 cloves garlic
680g jar of passata
50ml water
Handful fresh basil, torn
Salt and pepper to season
1 tsp dried chilli flakes (optional)
400g dried linguine

1. Wash the prepared calamari and slice into 2.5cm pieces.
2. Add the olive oil to a saucepan and heat to a moderate temperature. Add the calamari and stir whilst cooking for a further minute.
3. Crush the garlic and add to the calamari along with a pinch of salt.
4. Pour in the passata along with the water and stir.
5. Tear in a generous amount of basil, stir and leave to simmer for 1 hour 25 minutes.
6. 15 minutes before the sauce is ready, cook the linguine in salted water according to the packet instructions.
7. Drain the linguine and add a little sauce to colour the golden strands.
8. Spoon the linguine into bowls then gently arrange the calamari over and through the pasta and serve with freshly baked bread and lots of the sauce.

Ditalini with Peas
Pasta e piselli

Any small pasta can be used here, but ditalini are my favourite. They are small tubes also described as delicate thimbles – a very beautiful and quaint description. Pasta e piselli is a light pasta soup; in fact sometimes I simply cook the ditalini in a little stock with a handful of peas and nothing more, to make a very quick lunch or speedy dinner.

Preparation time: 5 minutes
Cooking time: 15 minutes
Serves: 4

2 tbsp olive oil
1 medium onion, finely chopped
1 garlic clove, crushed
225g peas
Salt and pepper to season
1.5 litres vegetable stock
450g ditalini pasta
50g parsley, chopped
30g pecorino, grated

1. Heat the olive oil in a frying pan and fry the onion gently with the crushed garlic for 4 minutes, until softened but not coloured.
2. Tumble in the peas, cook for 4 minutes and stir. Season with salt and pepper.
3. Add the onions and peas to the vegetable stock in a saucepan and bring the pan to a simmer.
4. Add the ditalini to the pan and cook according to the packet instructions, ensuring you keep the pasta al dente.
5. Add the chopped parsley and check for further seasoning.
6. Serve in warm bowls with a scattering of pecorino.

Carmela's tip
For added heat, sprinkle in a few flakes of dried chilli or fry a little pancetta with the onions to add flavour and texture.

Macaroni with Chickpeas

Pasta e ceci

A life without pasta would be like living a life without love, it is simply not possible. Here is another fabulous staple meal using everyday ingredients from the fridge and larder. To add a little more depth you can halve the quantity of chickpeas and substitute an equal amount of cannellini beans.

Preparation time: 10 minutes
Cooking time: 20 minutes
Serves: 4

3 tbsp olive oil
1 small onion, chopped
2 cloves garlic, crushed
200g pancetta, small cubes
4 tbsp tomato purée
1.5 litres chicken stock
400g can chickpeas
350g elbow macaroni, or penne
2 tbsp basil
2 tbsp parsley
Pepper to season
30g Parmesan, grated

1. Add the olive oil to a large pan and gently fry the onion and garlic for 5 minutes, taking care not to burn the garlic.
2. Scatter in the pancetta and cook on a medium heat for 6-8 minutes, then squeeze in the tomato purée and stir.
3. Tumble in the chickpeas with the juice from the can and stir. Add the chopped herbs to the pan and season with pepper.
4. Crush a few of the chickpeas with a fork to add a little texture to the dish.
5. Cook the pasta in the chicken stock until al dente.
6. Add the pasta and 4—6 ladles of stock into the pan with the pancetta and chickpeas, taste for seasoning and stir.
7. Serve in a warm bowl with a generous sprinkling of Parmesan.

Pasta from Beautiful Sorrento
Penne alla Sorrentina

After my recent visit to Sorrento I just had to try the regional dish of pasta alla Sorrentina. A rich and yet delicate tomato-based sauce with penne and stringy fresh moreish mozzarella. I have replicated this dish so many times since my return, I feel like a little part of Sorrento has come home with me.

Preparation time: 10 minutes
Cooking time: 25 minutes
Serves: 4–6

550g ripe tomatoes
4 tbsp olive oil
2 cloves garlic, finely sliced
1 tsp dried oregano
350g penne
300g mozzarella, sliced
50g Parmesan, grated
Large bunch basil, chopped
Salt and pepper to taste

1. Preheat the oven to 190°C (gas 5).
2. Score the bottom of the tomatoes with a knife and place in a pan of boiling water for 2 minutes.
3. Remove the tomatoes from the water with a slotted spoon and drop straight into a bowl of cold water to prevent further cooking and retain the colour.
4. Peel the skin from the tomatoes, remove the seeds and chop up roughly.
5. Add the oil to a frying pan and gently fry the garlic for 2 minutes.
6. Tumble in the tomatoes and season with oregano, salt and pepper. Stir and cook for 15 minutes.
7. Cook the penne in salted water until just al dente.
8. Add the penne to the tomatoes and add the sliced mozzarella. Stir the basil through.
9. Place into an ovenproof dish and sprinkle over the grated Parmesan.
10. Bake for 10 minutes until the mozzarella has just melted.

Orecchiette Pasta with Turnip Tops

Orecchiette con cime di rapa

Orecchiette is the regional pasta from Puglia and Basilicata. Little cap-shaped shells also known as little ears, orecchiette are still made by hand on the streets of Puglia, by nonnas and mothers teaching and encouraging their children to continue the traditions of old. Orecchiette are a challenge to make and it takes a little practice to master the perfect capped shape. Thank goodness we can buy them dried. Nonna Carmela is still trying to teach me, however I think she may have secretly given up now!

Preparation time: 15 minutes
Cooking time: 15 minutes
Serves: 4

500g orecchiette, dried or fresh
3 tbsp olive oil
2 cloves of garlic, sliced
Salt and pepper to season
1.5kg turnip tops, washed and trimmed
Pinch of dried chilli
30g Parmesan, grated

1. Cook the pasta according to the packet instructions in salted boiling water.
2. In a frying pan cook the olive oil and garlic, stirring, for 2 minutes.
3. Tumble in the chopped and prepared turnip tops and stir. Season with salt, pepper and a little chilli. Cook for 7 minutes on a gentle heat.
4. Once the pasta is al dente, drain it and add it to the turnip tops, then stir to combine.
5. Serve in a bowl with a generous grating of Parmesan.

Carmela's tip

If turnip tops are difficult to come by then use escarole, kale or cavolo nero. If you want to make your own orecchiette, use an eggless pasta dough made with semolina flour and water. You roll the pasta dough into long thin sausages and then cut a small piece of dough off the end, drag the dough over a wooden board using a rounded knife and then roll it over your thumb to create the rounded 'ear' shape.

Pasta Shells Filled with Ricotta and Mozzarella

Conchiglioni ripiene con ricotta e mozzarella

This recipe is one of my mother Solidea's trump cards and one of my family's favourite baked pasta dishes. The conchiglioni – large shells that are filled and baked in the oven – is so warming and is a complete meal in itself and we often have this meal as a weekend lunch. The pork mince can be easily changed to spinach to make a vegetarian version.

Preparation time: 25 minutes
Cooking time: 60 minutes
Serves: 6

500g conchiglioni (large) shells
500g minced pork
500g mozzarella, grated or chopped
500g ricotta
100g Parmesan, grated
3 cloves garlic, crushed
Salt and pepper to season
3 large eggs
4 tbsp parsley, chopped
400ml meat ragu sauce (page 34)
Oven dish 30cm x 30cm

1. Preheat the oven to 190°C (gas 5).
2. Brown off the minced pork in a frying pan and, when coloured, drain off any excess fat.
3. Place a large pan of water on to boil for the pasta shells, once the water is bubbling add 1 tbsp salt. Cook the conchiglioni shells for 9–10 minutes (3 minutes less than the packet instructions specify).
4. For the filling, combine the mozzarella, ricotta, Parmesan, garlic, salt and pepper and mix well. Add three large eggs and stir. Now add the pork that has been drained of fat and cooled slightly. Scatter in the chopped parsley and stir again.

5. Add 2 ladles of the ragu sauce to the filling so that it adds colour and a little texture to the mixture. Stir to combine.
6. In a 30cm x 30cm ovenproof dish, spoon two small ladles of sauce to cover the base.
7. Drain the conchiglioni shells then begin to fill them with the filling and place into the dish. Once the whole dish is bursting with shells, pour over a couple of ladles of sauce.
8. Cover the pasta with foil and bake for 45 minutes, then remove the foil and cook for a further 15 minutes until bubbling, golden and ready to enjoy.
9. Serve on warmed plates with a basket of fresh bread and a seasonal salad.

Pasta Shells with Butter and Pancetta

Conchigliette con burro e pancetta

Small pasta shells with browned butter and pancetta – speedy, inexpensive, easy and oh, so tasty. Southern Italy is all about eating well for less, using the store cupboard to produce a family meal for a minimum cost. You can change the shape of pasta, but always choose a shape that can hold the butter and pancetta.

Preparation time: 5 minutes
Cooking time: 10 minutes
Serves: 4

400g conchigliette (tiny pasta shells)
125g unsalted butter, cubed
250g pancetta, sliced or cubed
1 tbsp parsley, chopped
Salt and pepper to season

1. Three quarters fill a saucepan with water, bring to the boil and salt the water.
2. Cook the pasta according to the packet instructions, minus 2 minutes, keeping the pasta al dente.
3. In a frying pan add the cubed butter and fry the pancetta until it is lightly golden, for around 5-7 minutes.
4. Drain the pasta and tumble into the frying pan. Season with pepper and sprinkle over the chopped parsley, then stir to combine the pasta with the sauce.
5. Serve in warm bowls.

Pasta with Cannellini Beans

Pasta e fagiole

Known as peasant food and adored by all who have tried it, this dish is fresh, quick and inexpensive. I just love the style of cooking from the south of Italy, it really is *cucina povera* at its best, plus if you are looking for fast food, this is hard to beat. For the perfect filling dish ready in 30 minutes, here is mia mamma's version of pasta e fagiole.

Preparation time: 10 minutes
Cooking time: 30 minutes
Serves: 4

2 tbsp olive oil
200g pancetta, cubed
1 garlic clove, crushed
2 x 400g tins cannellini beans, in water
2 tbsp tomato purée
1 tsp chilli
3 tbsp basil, chopped
1 chicken stock cube
175g ditalini pasta (or any small shaped pasta)

1. Fry the pancetta and garlic for around 5 minutes in a saucepan with the olive oil.
2. Tumble in both tins of cannellini beans with the juice and add a further tin full of water.
3. Stir well and add the tomato purée, chilli, basil and stock cube. Stir well and cook for 25 minutes.
4. Add the uncooked pasta to the sauce 8 minutes before the cannellini beans are ready and cook until the pasta is al dente. Taste and season with salt and pepper if required.
5. Serve in a warm bowl with fresh bread.

Pasta with Potatoes

Pasta e patate

If you were to ask my father if he enjoys a bowl of pasta e patate I think he would become pale faced and run and hide in my Nonno Giuseppe's wine shed, as he used to 50 years ago. Clearly not one of his favourites, but the rest of my family absolutely loves it. A warm bowl of love and classic *cucina povera* food. If you have no fresh tomatoes then substitute 200g of tinned cherry tomatoes. Any small pasta works well in this dish.

Preparation time: 10 minutes
Cooking time: 30 minutes
Serves: 4

550g potatoes, peeled and cut into small cubes
300g ditalini (small tube-shaped pasta)
3 tbsp olive oil
100g pancetta
1 garlic clove, crushed
1 small onion, finely chopped
175g cherry tomatoes, halved
Small bunch celery leaves, finely chopped
½ tsp chilli
Salt and pepper to season
Small bunch basil, chopped
30g Parmesan

1. Take a large pan of water, lightly salt it and add the potatoes. Bring to the boil and simmer for 8 minutes, then tumble in the pasta and cook till al dente.
2. Whilst the potatoes are cooking, take a large sauté pan and fry the pancetta, garlic and onions gently in the oil for 10 minutes.
3. Tumble in the halved tomatoes and cook for a further 5 minutes.
4. The tomatoes will begin to soften so push them down with the back of a wooden spoon. Add the celery leaves and stir, then sprinkle in the chilli.

5. Drain the pasta and potatoes (reserve three ladles of the cooking water) and stir them into the pan with the reserved cooking water. Season with salt and pepper and scatter over the fresh herbs.
6. Serve in warm bowls with a generous grating of Parmesan.

Carmela's tip

To add a contrast of texture you can tumble in a tin of cannellini beans along with a tin of chick peas.

Penne with Chilli and Garlic
Penne arrabbiata

Everyone has dried pasta in the larder and penne is definitely one of the most popular types. Penne is wonderful because the sauce finds its own way into the centre of the pasta tube, holding its flavour with every bite. Here is another recipe made within minutes from your home store cupboard. There is no need for fresh tomatoes, as the tinned variety work perfectly in this speedy and extremely tasty dish.

Preparation time: 5 minutes
Cooking time: 12 minutes
Serves: 4

5 tbsp olive oil
2 garlic cloves, crushed
1 medium red chilli, seeds removed and finely chopped
2 x 400g tins chopped tomatoes
2 tbsp flat leaf parsley, chopped
3 tbsp Parmesan, grated
500g penne
Salt and pepper to season

1. Bring a large pan of water to the boil for the pasta. Salt the water well.
2. In a frying pan pour in the oil and add the crushed garlic and chilli. Cook for 1 minute and stir.
3. Add the chopped tomatoes to the chilli and garlic and season with salt and pepper. Cook on a medium heat for a further 10 minutes.
4. Add the penne to the boiling water and cook according to the packet instructions. Ensure the pasta is still left with a bite (al dente).
5. Once the pasta is cooked, drain it and tip it into the tomato sauce and stir.
6. Serve in warm bowls and scatter over the parsley together with a generous handful of grated Parmesan.

Rocco's Spaghetti with Garlic and Oil

Spaghetti aglio e olio

This may have been the first dish that my father Rocco learnt to cook and he is still incredibly proud to be able to cook a delicious bowl of relatively simple yet incredibly satisfying spaghetti. Said to have originated from the region of Abruzzo, Spaghetti aglio e olio is made throughout Italy and due to its simplicity and convenience makes a wonderful *cucina povera* dish. It's ready in just the time it takes for the spaghetti to cook.

Preparation time: 5 minutes
Cooking time: 11 minutes
Serves: 4

400g spaghetti
6–8 tbsp extra virgin olive oil
2 garlic cloves, sliced
1 small chilli,
2 tbsp flat leaf parsley, chopped
Salt and pepper

1. Three quarters fill a large saucepan with water and place on the stove.
2. Salt the water well once it begins to boil then cook the spaghetti according to the packet instructions minus 2 minutes, keeping the spaghetti al dente.
3. In a frying pan, heat the olive oil and fry the garlic until it is lightly golden, do not let it burn. Add the chilli and stir.
4. Once the spaghetti is cooked, drain and tumble into the frying pan. Toss well, season with salt and pepper and sprinkle with chopped parsley.
5. Serve in warmed pasta bowls.

Potato Dumplings

Gnocchi

Gnocchi are a delicious alternative to pasta. Gnocchi that have been made fresh are truly amazing and light, where I find dried gnocchi that you can purchase in supermarkets are dense and a little heavy. The reason why I love to make gnocchi and pasta by hand at home is that I really find it relaxing. I immerse myself completely. This recipe is a basic gnocchi recipe and you can add more flavours, spices and varied cheeses into the potato mix. The gnocchi are best eaten fresh with a sauce of your choice and lots of freshly grated Parmesan or pecorino.

Preparation time: 15 minutes
Cooking time: 25 minutes
Serves: 4–6

1 kg potatoes
1 egg
250g '00' flour
Salt and pepper to season
50g polenta grain

1. Take a large saucepan and three quarters fill it with water. Bring the water to the boil and add the potatoes with their skins on. Cook the potatoes until tender. The skins are left on the potatoes so no water is able to penetrate through and affect the consistency of the potato.
2. Once the potatoes are ready, drain and allow them to cool slightly, then peel them. Pass the potatoes through a potato ricer to ensure there are no lumps or mash them thoroughly if you don't have a potato ricer. Place the potatoes in a large bowl once riced.
3. Crack the egg into the potatoes and add half the flour. Season with salt and pepper.
4. Use a wooden spoon to work the potato mix into a dough, then use your hands to continue to bring it together.

5. Lightly flour a wooden board and tumble out the dough. Work the remaining flour into the dough, kneading with your hands.
6. Separate the dough into workable portions and roll out each portion into long sausages. Cut the sausages into bite-sized gnocchi.
7. Once cut to size, sit the gnocchi on a scattering of polenta to prevent them from sticking.
8. You can roll a fork over the gnocchi to make indentations in the top or use a gnocchi board. A simple roll over will develop ridges therefore ensuring the gnocchi holds the sauce you serve it with.
9. Bring a pan of salted water to a rolling boil – a state of continuous rapid boiling. In batches, gently drop in the freshly made gnocchi for about 3–4 minutes, until they rise up to the surface of the water. Use a slotted spoon to remove the gnocchi.
10. Serve with a simple browned butter or extra virgin olive oil and grated Parmesan.

Carmela's tip

My favourite way to serve this dish is to run some tomato sauce through the gnocchi and place them gently into an ovenproof dish. Sprinkle with a little Parmesan and generously scatter over some chopped mozzarella and basil. Place under a grill for five minutes until the mozzarella has melted.

Spinach and Ricotta Ravioli
Ravioli con spinaci e ricotta

A pillow of pasta filled with an incredible and very traditional flavour, ravioli can be filled with anything from thyme and mushrooms, sun dried tomato and Parma ham, butternut squash and mascarpone, to my favourite – ricotta and spinach with a pinch of nutmeg.

Preparation time: 30 minutes
Cooking time: 10 minutes
Serves: 4

300g ricotta
350g spinach
80g pecorino
Salt and pepper, to season
½ tsp nutmeg, grated
400g prepared pasta dough (page 138)
30g polenta

1. Crumble the ricotta into a mixing bowl using a fork. Wilt the spinach in the microwave for 30 seconds or pour over boiling water from a kettle, leave for 2 minutes then drain any excess water. Squeeze the spinach well. I place the leaves into a clean tea towel and squeeze excess moisture out.
2. Chop the spinach and add it to the ricotta cheese. Sprinkle in the pecorino, season with salt and pepper, add the grated nutmeg and mix well.
3. Take your prepared dough and halve it, this will make it easier to pass through the pasta machine. Roll out half the dough, following the instructions for simple pasta dough on page 138.
4. Once you have reached the correct thickness (normally the setting before last on your pasta machine) flour your board.

5. Lay the pasta sheets out on your board and spoon teaspoon amounts of the filling onto one side of the dough, leaving a 3cm gap in between each spoonful. Brush between the filling with a little water and fold the dough lengthways. Repeat with the remaining sheets of dough.
6. Seal each raviolo by pressing the dough together with your fingers, taking care to remove any air bubbles as you work, so the ravioli do not pop and open in the pan. Cut between the moulded ravioli using either a pasta wheel or pastry cutter. Sprinkle the parcels with polenta or semolina to prevent them from sticking and set aside until you are ready to cook.
7. Cook the ravioli in salted boiling water for 3–4 minutes.
8. Serve with a tomato ragu or warmed butter and sage sauce.

Spaghetti Carbonara

Spaghetti alla carbonara

Authentic and traditional spaghetti alla carbonara. By the time the spaghetti is cooked the sauce is ready. Never add cream to a carbonara – the sauce is already velvety and rich. All you need are basic store cupboard ingredients to quickly prepare the most delicious of family meals.

Preparation time: 5 minutes
Cooking time: 12 minutes
Serves: 4

500g packet spaghetti
4 tbsp olive oil
400g pancetta, cubed
2 cloves garlic, crushed
70g Parmesan, grated (plus a little extra for topping)
1 large egg plus 3 egg yolks
1 tbsp parsley, chopped
Salt and pepper
1 tbsp basil, chopped

1. Cook the spaghetti according to the packet instructions in salted boiling water.
2. Fry the pancetta in a little olive oil with the crushed garlic until coloured.
3. In a bowl mix the cheese, whole egg and yolks together and season with salt and pepper and add the chopped parsley.
4. Drain the spaghetti and add it to the pancetta and garlic, then stir well. Stir the egg sauce into the spaghetti and add the chopped basil.
5. The heat of the pancetta and spaghetti will cook the egg mixture as you stir.
6. Serve in large bowls with the reserved grated Parmesan sprinkled over the top.

Spaghetti with Baby Plum Tomatoes

Spaghetti con pomodorini

A wonderful light dish, perfect to cook and prepare in the height of summer, using an abundance of cherry or plum tomatoes that have been sweating in the midday heat. Tomatoes will add instant colour, sweetness and flavour to the simplest of dishes. This one is simple and fast – ready in just 15 minutes.

Preparation time: 10 minutes
Cooking time: 15 minutes
Serves: 4

500g packet spaghetti
6 tbsp olive oil
2 garlic cloves, crushed
15 baby plum tomatoes on the vine, quartered
Large handful fresh basil, torn
30g olives, pips removed and halved
Salt and pepper to season
100ml reserved pasta water
40g pecorino, grated

1. Place a pan of water on to boil. Once boiling, salt well and add the spaghetti to cook. Cook the spaghetti according to the packet instructions.
2. In a frying pan heat a large glug of olive oil then add the crushed garlic. Fry for 2 minutes then add the baby tomatoes and cook until they start to burst.
3. When the tomatoes become soft squash them down with a fork and stir. Add the halved olives and season with salt and pepper.
4. Add half the basil to the tomatoes and stir.
5. Once the spaghetti is cooked, lift it out of the water and place it directly into the frying pan with the tomato sauce and mix. Pour in 100ml of the cooking water from the spaghetti and mix. Sprinkle in the remaining basil, stir and add the grated pecorino, toss and serve.

Spaghetti with Broccoli and Toasted Breadcrumbs

Spaghetti con broccoli e pangrattato

If you are making this dish for your children then be a little wary of the amount of chilli you use. If made in advance with penne pasta and allowed to cool, it makes a great alternative for children's lunchboxes. I also like to use sprouting broccoli when it is in season and cavolo nero to add a depth of colour and a change of flavour. A wonderful addition to the dish is the pangrattato, which is toasted seasoned breadcrumbs that are scattered on top of the finished dish.

Preparation time: 15 minutes
Cooking time: 20 minutes
Serves: 4

2 slices sourdough bread
2 tbsp olive oil
Small bunch parsley
300g stem broccoli
300g spaghetti
4 tbsp olive oil
3 anchovy fillets, fincly chopped
1 garlic clove, finely sliced
1 small red chilli, finely chopped
30g Parmesan, grated

1. Preheat the oven to 190°C (gas 5).
2. Cube the bread and place on a baking tray with a drizzle of olive oil. Bake for 10–15 minutes.
3. Place the bread in a food processor along with the parsley and blitz, then tip into a bowl and set aside.
4. Bring a large saucepan of water to the boil and salt the water.
5. Add the broccoli and cook for 4 minutes until just tender. Using a slotted spoon remove the broccoli and set aside.

6. In the same water as the broccoli, cook the spaghetti according to the packet instructions.
7. In a frying pan add 2 tbsp olive oil along with the garlic, anchovies and chilli, fry gently for 2 minutes. Tumble in the broccoli and stir.
8. When the pasta is ready, drain and add to the frying pan and stir. Drizzle over the remaining olive oil and serve in bowls with a sprinkle of pangrattato on top and a generous amount of Parmesan.

Spinach and Ricotta Gnocchi
Gnocchi con spinaci e ricotta

Gnocchi should be light and fluffy. They are not dense or heavy, but are simply delicious and melt in the mouth. These are made without potato, but are just as delightful as potato gnocchi (page 158). When you have more spinach than you know what to do with, this is a perfect way to use it up, mixed with fresh ricotta cheese and fragrant nutmeg.

Preparation time: 30 minutes
Cooking time: 10 minutes
Serves: 4

200g spinach, washed
Small bunch parsley, chopped
1 garlic clove, crushed
150g fresh ricotta
90g '00' flour
2 medium eggs
100g Parmesan, grated
Salt and pepper to season
Nutmeg, grated

1. Begin by wilting the spinach. The easiest way to do this is to cook it in the microwave for 1 minute. Drain and squeeze any remaining liquid from the spinach.
2. Chop up the spinach with the parsley and place in a large bowl.
3. Add the crushed garlic, ricotta, flour, eggs and Parmesan to the bowl. Stir through using a fork.
4. Season with salt, pepper and a generous grating of nutmeg. Stir to incorporate fully.
5. Use damp hands to form walnut-size balls of gnocchi, then place them on a tray or plate and allow to chill in the fridge for at least 30 minutes or up to 24 hours.

6. When you are ready to cook, bring a large pan of water up to boil. The gnocchi needs to be added to the pan in batches of 8–10 at a time once the salted water has reached a rolling boil – continuous rapid boiling.
7. The gnocchi will sink immediately and will pop up to the surface once they are ready. Allow them to cook for a further minute before removing with a slotted spoon.
8. Set them aside while you cook the remaining gnocchi.
9. Serve in warm bowls with a drizzle of extra virgin olive oil and freshly grated Parmesan.

Carmela's tip
I love gnocchi with a simple tomato sauce.

Sunday Lasagne
Lasagne per la famiglia

Traditionally, the meal that brings our famiglia together on a Sunday is lasagne. This is the recipe that I have been eating and serving for many years, taught to me by my mum Solidea. The recipe below makes a large lasagne to feed ten to twelve people, depending on appetite. Remember, any leftovers can be portioned and popped into the deep freeze or the recipe can simply be halved. This is a dish that still brings a smile to my face – I hope you enjoy it.

Preparation time: 40 minutes
Cooking time: 4 hours 30 minutes
Serves: 10–12

For the sauce (sugo):
700g pork mince
700g beef mince
4 x 680g passata
3 garlic cloves, crushed
100g tomato purée
300ml water
Handful of basil
For the lasagne:
6 eggs, hardboiled
2 eggs, beaten
18 fresh lasagne sheets
500g mozzarella, grated
80g Parmesan, grated

1. Start by making the sugo. Fry the mince in a large saucepan for approximately 5–7 minutes, until it is browned.
2. Add the garlic and tomato purée, and stir.
3. Pour in the passata along with the water and stir again then season with salt and pepper. Scatter over the basil and simmer for 2 hours 30 minutes.
4. When the sugo is ready, preheat the oven to 170°C (gas 4) and start to assemble the lasagne. You will need a large ovenproof dish, 30cm x 40cm.

5. Chop the eggs.
6. Ladle 3 spoonfuls of passata mince into the ovenproof dish and place a layer of lasagne pasta sheets on top.
7. Sprinkle over some mozzarella, chopped egg and, using a fork, drizzle over some of the beaten egg to bind the filling.
8. Repeat this process layer by layer. Finish the lasagne with a layer of mince sauce and a grating of mozzarella. Sprinkle over the Parmesan.
9. Cover with foil and bake for 1 hour 30 minutes. Remove the foil and cook for a further 15 minutes to allow the lasagne to brown.
10. Switch off the oven and let the lasagne stand for 15 minutes before slicing. I find that the best way to do this is to leave the lasagne in the oven but with the door held slightly ajar.
11. Serve with a seasonal side salad.

Carmela's tip

You can cut down the cooking time considerably if you make the sugo a day or so in advance.

Tiny Pasta with Egg

Pastina con uova

Pastina was a staple meal in our home growing up and likewise still is for my children. My mother Solidea would always make a bowl for my sister Daniela and I when we were poorly. It's the Italian take on a chicken soup, warming yet light. This tiny pasta is used with a chicken stock, again simple cooking at its best. You can add a ladle of passata to the stock so the soup changes colour, however an alternative is to crack in an egg two minutes before serving and stir.

Preparation time: 5 minutes
Cooking time: 10 minutes
Serves: 4

1.7 litres chicken stock
2 tbsp basil, chopped
350g pastina
2 large eggs

1. Bring the chicken stock to a gentle simmer and add the fresh basil.
2. Tumble in the pastina and stir. Cook according to the packet instructions, taking care to keep the pastina al dente – with a bite to it.
3. Crack the eggs into the pastina 2 minutes before it is ready and stir continuously until the eggs are cooked and the pastina is ready.
4. Ladle into bowls and serve with bread.

Risotto and Polenta

Risotto can be a warming and 'blanket over the knee' comforting dish. To make risotto you need a little time, a wooden spoon, some patient slow stirring and a large glass of vino. A good quality hot stock is essential, then all you need to do is add some robust flavours to a simple risotto rice to make a delicious one-bowl meal. The north of Italy boasts large areas of paddy fields, growing short-grained rice, which is used in risotto and often to fill vegetables, such as tomatoes and peppers as opposed to being eaten as a side dish, which is how it is served in many other countries. There are four categories of risotto rice, and they are all characterised by their size, shape and length. There are numerous varieties, too. Arborio is the best-known variety outside Italy and is commonly found in all supermarkets, but the more expensive carnaroli and vialone nano are the most highly regarded in Italy and can be found in most Italian delis in the UK.

Polenta is a yellow, gluten-free grain used in savoury and sweet dishes. Soft cooked as a base for beans and various cuts of meat, I also use polenta for the base of my polenta pizza on page 180.

Italian Sausage with Cannellini Beans and Polenta
Salsicce con cannelini e polenta

This dish is comfort in a bowl. Warming, a little stodgy (in a good way) and completely tummy filling. It's a perfect evening meal. Soft sausages with the tomatoes seem to welcome the warm bed of amber polenta, but a little bread for dipping is a must, too, so remember to place your bread basket on the table.

Preparation time: 10 minutes
Cooking time: 30 minutes
Serves: 4–6

For the sauce:
12 soft Italian sausages
2 medium red onions, sliced
2 garlic cloves, crushed
1 large glass red wine
2 x 400g tins chopped tomatoes
1 x 400g tin cannellini beans, drained
4 sage leaves, sliced
Salt and pepper to season
Small bunch of parsley, chopped
For the polenta:
650ml water
150g polenta
Salt and pepper
50g Parmesan, grated
20g butter

1. In a large sauté pan, fry the sausages in a little oil until browned, then set aside.
2. Fry the onions in 1 tbsp oil for 5 minutes, scraping the bottom of the pan with a wooden spoon to release all the lovely sticky pieces left from the sausages.

3. Add the crushed garlic, cook for a further 2 minutes and add the red wine to deglaze the pan. Simmer for 4 minutes.
4. Add the 2 tins of chopped tomatoes, stir and season with salt and pepper. Place the sausages back into the pan, tumble in the cannellini beans and sprinkle over the sliced sage.
5. Place a lid on the pan and simmer away for 20 minutes.
6. Bring the water for the polenta to the boil and then lightly salt it. Add the polenta, stir vigorously with a wooden spoon and season with salt and pepper. The polenta will take about 4 minutes to cook. Scatter in the grated Parmesan, butter and stir. Once the polenta comes away clean from the pan it is ready to serve.
7. Spoon the warm polenta onto plates then serve the sausages and tomatoes over the top.

Pancetta, Broad Bean and Pea Risotto

Risotto con fava e pancetta

A wooden spoon in one hand and a glass of vino bianco in the other – both are key ingredients to a creamy risotto. Sweet peas and beans make a delicious contrast to the saltiness of the pancetta – this is a truly irresistible risotto.

Preparation time: 15 minutes
Cooking time: 25–30 minutes
Serves: 4

175g broad beans
125g peas
1.2 litres ready-made chicken stock (page 28)
2 tbsp olive oil
65g pancetta, sliced or cubed
1 garlic clove, peeled and crushed
2 shallots, finely chopped
240g risotto rice
70ml white wine
4 tbsp Parmesan, grated
20g butter

1. Take a small saucepan and half fill with water. Add the beans and peas to the water and cook for 3 minutes then drain and tumble into ice cold water to stop them cooking any more. Set aside until required.
2. Warm the chicken stock in a pan on the stove.
3. In a frying pan, heat a little oil and cook the pancetta gently for 3 minutes. Add the garlic and shallots, then fry gently for 5 minutes until soft and translucent.
4. Tip in the rice and stir, allowing each grain to become coated with the oil and vegetables. Pour in the white wine and stir again.

5. Gradually you need to add the stock; do this a ladle at a time, and stir. Keep stirring and adding stock, allowing the rice to absorb the stock each time before you add the next ladle. Keep going until the rice is cooked and you have used all the stock. This will take around 20 minutes.
6. Add the beans and peas when the rice is almost tender and cook for a further 2 minutes.
7. Remove from the heat, add the grated Parmesan and stir in the butter.

Carmela's tip
Frozen beans and peas would work well out of season.

Risotto with Mushrooms
Risotto con fungi

Autumn is the perfect time to go foraging for mushrooms (fungi); however I do not trust myself at all so I buy mine safely from the greengrocers. Never pick wild fungi unless you are completely sure that they are an edible variety. Shops sell such a wide range of interesting mushrooms now, that there is no need to risk disaster by foraging for something unusual.

Preparation time: 10 minutes
Cooking time: 30 minutes
Serves: 4–6

1.5 litres chicken or vegetable stock
2 tbsp olive oil
1 medium onion, finely chopped
1 garlic clove, finely chopped
1 stick celery, finely chopped
400g carnaroli rice
1 large glass white wine
125g mixed mushrooms, cleaned and chopped (chestnut, portobello, enoke, porchini)
1 lemon, zested
Small sprig thyme and extra for garnish
30g Parmesan, grated
25g butter, cubed

1. Heat the stock and leave it simmering at the back of the stove. This could be a prepared stock (page 28 or 40) or good quality stock cubes are also fine.
2. Place a large shallow pan or frying pan over a medium heat and add a little olive oil followed by the onion, garlic and celery. Cook for 5–8 minutes until softened and translucent.
3. In a separate frying pan heat 10g butter and 2 tbsp olive oil. Tumble in the mushrooms and season with salt and pepper. Scatter over the thyme and cook slowly for 10 minutes.

4. Scatter the rice into the celery pan and stir, coating every grain with the soffritto mixture.
5. Pour in the white wine, stir and cook for 4 minutes, until the rice has absorbed the liquid.
6. Then start to add the stock, a ladle at a time. This will allow the rice to absorb the stock slowly. Remember, be patient.
7. Add the first ladle of stock. Stir constantly until the stock has reduced by three quarters then add another, remembering to stir again.
8. Carry on adding stock to the rice until the rice is cooked but still has a bite and is al dente, this may take 25 minutes or so.
9. 5 minutes before serving, scatter over the mushrooms, lemon zest, Parmesan, thyme, butter and a generous grind of salt and pepper.
10. Stir them into the risotto and serve in warm bowls with a drizzle of extra virgin olive oil and a few thyme leaves.

Risotto with Peas

Risotto con piselli

This is a very simple risotto, and an ideal recipe to begin with. You start by making a soffritto – onion, celery and garlic, cooked down in a little olive oil – which is the basis of many Italian dishes. You can make your own stock (pages 28 and 40) for this recipe, or just use stock made from a good quality stock cube or stock pot.

Preparation time: 10 minutes
Cooking time: 30 minutes
Serves: 4–6

1.5 litres chicken or vegetable stock
Olive oil
1 onion, finely chopped
1 garlic clove, finely chopped
1 stick celery, finely chopped
400g risotto rice
1 large glass white wine
70g peas
1 lemon, zested
4 mint leaves, sliced
Leafy celery top, chopped
30g Parmesan, grated
15g butter

1. Heat the stock and leave it simmering at the back of the stove.
2. Place a large shallow pan or frying pan over a medium heat and add a little olive oil followed by the onion, garlic and celery. Cook for 5-8 minutes until softened and translucent.
3. Scatter in the rice and stir, coating every grain with the soffritto mixture.
4. Pour in the white wine, stir and cook for 4 minutes until all the liquid has been absorbed.

5. The stock must be added to the risotto a ladle at a time. This will allow the rice to absorb the stock slowly. Remember, be patient.

6. Add the first ladle of stock. Stir constantly until the stock has reduced by three quarters then add another, remembering to stir again.

7. Carry on adding stock to the rice until the rice is cooked but still has a bite and is al dente, this may take 25 minutes or so.

8. 5 minutes before serving, add the peas, zest, mint, celery tops, Parmesan, butter and a generous grind of salt and pepper. Stir well.

9. Serve in warm bowls with a drizzle of extra virgin olive oil.

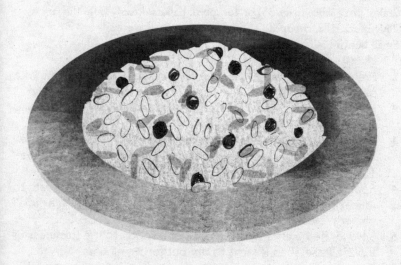

Polenta Pizza

Pizza di polenta

Polenta is a coarse grain, similar to couscous, that absorbs flavours and works best with herbs and flavoured stocks. On its own, it is bland. Any Italian meal will begin with pasta, rice or polenta – a cheap but filling dish that minimises the quantity of fish and meat that would otherwise be required. Here, the polenta makes a base for a pizza, ready from start to finish in just 15 minutes. The consistency of the base is soft with the polenta but light to bite. Thank you again to Nonna Carmela for this beautiful *cucina povera* recipe.

Preparation time: 10 minutes
Cooking time: 8–10 minutes
Serves: 4

800ml vegetable stock
200g instant polenta grain
1 tsp dried oregano
Salt and pepper
200ml pizza sauce (page 35) or, for speed, passata directly from the jar
250g mozzarella, chopped
Small bunch basil, torn

1. Preheat the oven to 190°C (gas 5) and line 2 baking sheets with parchment paper.
2. Pour the stock into a saucepan and season with a little salt and pepper and bring to a light simmer.
3. Pour in the polenta and half of the oregano. Stir with a wooden spoon for about 3 minutes keeping the saucepan on the heat. The polenta will thicken very quickly.
4. Spoon the polenta onto one of the prepared baking sheets to make 4 pizza bases, each approximately the size of a small dinner plate, about 20cm in diameter.
5. Spread the polenta with the back of a spoon to the thickness of a pizza base, then leave it to dry out for 10 minutes.
6. Spoon over the pizza sauce, top with mozzarella and a scattering of basil and the remaining dried oregano.
7. Bake for 10 minutes then serve with a leafy rocket salad.

Biscotti, Cakes and Desserts

There is always room for a little something sweet after any Italian meal. Whether some seasonal, chopped fresh fruit or a full-on panna cotta, tiramisu or sorbet. I would be doing desserts an injustice if I didn't talk about gelato (ice cream). Perhaps I am a little biased but I have to say that gelato from any Italian gelateria is the best and is certainly a delicious treat that Italians should be incredibly proud of.

A sfogliatelle is a filled pastry with an Italian cream or a sponge soaked in rum (baba) which will definitely leave you with a smile on your face. There is nothing better than visiting a pasticceria, an Italian pastry shop, where you can peruse the array of cakes and biscotti on offer whilst indulging in a fresh espresso.

When in season and at its best, it would not be uncommon to find a large bowl of quartered fennel on any Italian table. Not only is it fresh and cleansing on the palate after a rich meal, but it is also essential in aiding digestion.

Ciambella Cake

Ciambella

Ciambella is a circular cake traditionally made at Easter. When I think of ciambella I immediately think of my Nonna Carmela, who would make one for me whenever I visited. Ciambella has a wonderful hit of a spirit called strega, which is flavoured with saffron. There is also another special ingredient added to this cake, called 'pane di angeli'. This is a combination of baking powder and vanilla, used very often in Italian baking, and can be bought from your local Italian deli.

Preparation time: 15 minutes
Cooking time: 50 minutes
Serves: 10-12

1 large lemon, zested
3 large eggs
Strega, 1 shot glass
1 large lemon, juiced
100ml warm milk
1 sachet pane di angeli
200g self-raising flour
200g caster sugar
150ml sunflower oil
10g icing sugar to dust

1. Grease and flour a 22cm round Savarin cake tin – a cake tin with a hole in the centre – and preheat the oven to 190°C (gas 5).
2. Zest the lemon and place the zest to one side.
3. Crack the eggs into a bowl along with the strega and juice of the lemon and whisk for 7 minutes until you have a light, fluffy mixture.
4. Warm the milk and stir in the pane di angeli until it becomes frothy.
5. Once the egg mixture is ready add the caster sugar and whisk, followed by the flour, oil, zest and milk mixture.

6. Combine fully and pour into your prepared cake tin and level. Bake until golden, approximately 50 minutes.

7. Allow the cake to sit in the tin for at least 10 minutes before turning out, then serve, sliced, with a dusting of icing sugar.

Carmela's tip

Pane di angeli can be purchased from Italian delicatessens. However 1 tsp baking powder and 2 tsp of vanilla extract will be fine in its place if you cannot find any in shops near you.

Coffee Granita

Granita al caffe

For a refreshing cooler in the midday sun, granita is the answer. The granita can be churned in an ice cream maker or simply made using your domestic freezer. Served in tall delicate glasses or tiny espresso cups, granita makes a thirst-quenching alternative to a glass of water.

Preparation time: 5 minutes
Serves: 4

125g caster sugar
200ml very strong espresso
175ml cold water

1. Dissolve the sugar in the hot coffee and stir.
2. Add the cold water, stir and allow to cool for 2 hours.
3. Pour the liquid into a shallow dish and place in the freezer.
4. Check every hour and, using a fork, break up the ice crystals. Repeat this process 4 times.
5. After 3 hours, fork through or blitz in a food processor.
6. Serve in tall elegant glasses.

Auntie Anna's Amaretto and Dark Chocolate Cake
Torta di chocolate e amaretto

Chocolate and amaretto paired together is a marriage made in food heaven. This is one of my Aunty Anna's cake recipes, although I have increased the amounts of amaretto liqueur and dark chocolate, and transported it into another, indulgent dimension. It's a family favourite in our home and it makes a perfect celebration cake with a layer of fresh amaretto cream slathered over the top.

Preparation time: 15 minutes
Cooking time: 50 minutes
Serves: 12

4 large eggs
50g caster sugar
200g softened butter
200g self-raising flour
100g ground almonds
1 sachet pane di angeli (see page 182)
30ml warm milk
200g dark chocolate, chopped
200g amaretto biscuits (the hard ones)
2 tbsp amaretto liqueur

1. Preheat the oven to 180°C (gas 4).
2. For this cake I like to use a large bowl and wooden spoon, not a mixer, as you need to retain the texture of the biscuits and chocolate. In a bowl crack the eggs and mix with the caster sugar and butter.
3. Chop the chocolate and bash the amaretto biscuits. The amaretto biscuits are ideal if they are smashed into uneven pieces. The best way to do this is to pop the biscuits into a bag and bash with a wooden spoon or rolling pin.
4. Add the flour and ground almonds into the eggs, sugar and butter mix and stir well.
5. Warm the milk, add the pane di angeli and mix well. Once it becomes frothy, pour it into the bowl.
6. Add the chocolate, amaretto biscuits, amaretto liqueur and stir well. The mixture will smell amazing at this point.
7. Pour the mixture into a greased and lined, loose-bottomed, 22cm cake tin, push down evenly and bake for approximately 50 minutes, until golden.

Fennel Biscuits

Taralle con finoccio

Taralle always remind me of Christmas and Easter. Times of excitement to come together and celebrate, of course involving a feast of various speciality foods. Nonna would send each of our families small bags with different flavoured taralle. Sweet taralle are slightly more rotund and the savoury taralle are slim and delicately formed. The fennel taralle are my favourite. They make a wonderful savoury snack, lightly bronzed, with a crumbly texture and a fantastic hint of aniseed. They are delicious dipped into a little vino rosso too.

Preparation time: 7 minutes
Cooking and drying time: 1 hour 40 minutes
Makes: 20–25

500g '00' flour
4 large eggs
60ml olive oil
1 tbsp salt
3 tsp fennel seeds

1. Tip the flour out onto a large wooden board in a heap and make a well in the centre. Crack in the eggs and add the olive oil and salt.
2. Sprinkle over the freckles of fennel seeds.
3. Slowly bring the flour into the eggs to form a dough. Work the mixture for approximately 5 minutes.
4. Split the dough in half and roll each half into two long sausages, approximately 25mm in diameter.
5. Pull off 15cm sections of dough and roll again if necessary to make a neat sausage, then bend it round to form an oval and push the ends securely together.
6. Carry on until all the dough has been used.
7. Take a large saucepan and three quarters fill it with water. Bring to a steady rolling boil – a continuous rapid boil.

8. Preheat the oven to 180°C (gas 4).
9. Gently lower five taralle at a time into the boiling water and allow to cook. When they rise up to the top of the water (around 4 minutes), turn them over with a slotted spoon and cook for a further 2 minutes. Then take them out carefully with a slotted spoon and place on a dry, clean tea towel. Repeat with all the taralle.
10. Leave the taralle on the tea towel to dry out for at least an hour, making sure to turn them after 30 minutes.
11. Place the taralle on two baking trays, making sure to space them out. Pop them into the oven for 15 minutes after which time they need to be turned and then returned to the oven for a further 3–5 minutes.
12. Remove and cool on a wire rack.

Carmela's tip

Stored in an airtight jar or container, the taralle will keep for up to 4 weeks, although I'm sure they will all be polished off long before then.

Lemon and Polenta Cake
Torta con limone e polenta

Polenta is an ingredient that has sustained Italian people and Italian food for so many years. It is inexpensive, filling, versatile and very delicious too, and is also known as cornmeal. Polenta gives a great denseness to a cake, but also the texture changes and you are left with a crumbly bite every time. Citrus fruit works incredibly well with polenta. I have previously made an orange and polenta cake with an orange drizzle, but this lemon cake needs no drizzle in my opinion as all of the lemony deliciousness has been added to the cake mix.

Preparation time: 10 minutes
Cooking time: 50 minutes–1 hour
Serves: 8–10

240g butter
200g golden caster sugar
3 eggs
260g self-raising flour
1 large lemon, zested and juiced
110g polenta grain
1 tsp demerara sugar

1. Preheat the oven to 170°C (gas 4). Grease and line a 900g (2lb) loaf tin.
2. Cream the butter and sugar for 4 minutes until light and pale in colour.
3. Add the eggs one at a time and stir. Every time you add an egg to the mix you also need to add 2 tbsp of flour from the 260g; this will prevent the mixture from splitting.
4. Once all the eggs have been incorporated, tip in the remaining flour and mix.
5. Add the zest and juice of your lemon and stir in the polenta.
6. Pour the mixture into the loaf tin, sprinkle the top of the cake with the demerara sugar and bake for 50 minutes to 1 hour.

Carmela's tip
This dense cake is delicious dipped into espresso coffee.

Summer Fruit Ice Cream
Semifreddo

Semifreddo is a semi-frozen dessert – always refreshing and scrumptious on a hot summer's day. I recommend lining the loaf tin with cling film to make it very easy to transfer onto a plate and slice. Studded with seasonal summer berries, I can't think of a more perfect after-dinner palate cleanser.

Preparation time: 15 minutes
Cooking time: 7 minutes
Serves: 6–8

250g raspberries
200g blueberries
6 tbsp granulated sugar
2 tbsp Chambord liquor (optional)
Juice of half a lemon
200ml double cream
200g Greek yogurt
Handful of berries, to serve

1. Tip the raspberries and blueberries into a food processor and blitz for 30 seconds. Alternatively, use a fork to mash them up a little in a mixing bowl.
2. Add the puréed fruit to a small saucepan and sprinkle over the sugar, Chambord (if using) and lemon juice. Stir and simmer over a low heat for 5–7 minutes until slightly syrupy.
3. In a separate bowl, whisk the cream to the texture of soft peaks and then fold in the Greek yogurt.
4. Push the syrupy fruit through a plastic sieve to remove seeds, which you can discard. Allow the fruit syrup to cool a little before stirring into the cream and yoghurt mixture.
5. Line a 2lb loaf tin with cling film, then pour in the mixture and freeze for a minimum of 4 hours.
6. Transfer to the fridge 30 minutes before serving. Remove from the loaf tin, slice and serve scattered with berries.

Limoncello Ice Cream
Limoncello gelato

This fabulous, grown-up gelato is quick to prepare and works well with homemade or shop bought limoncello. It is a lovely dessert at the end of a meal.

Preparation time: 10 minutes
Chilling time: 6 hours
Serves: 4–6

3 large unwaxed lemons, zest and juice
200g icing sugar
450ml whipping cream
4 tbsp limoncello

1. Zest and juice the lemons and place in a bowl. Stir in the icing sugar a little at a time.
2. Add the limoncello to the cream and whisk until firmly whipped. Add the lemon mixture and combine.
3. Transfer into a freezer container and freeze for at least 6 hours.
4. Serve in glasses, simple and refreshing.

Marsala and Egg Yolk Froth
Zabaglione

A light foam enhanced with a delicious marsala spirit, this was a very popular dessert in Italian restaurants in the 1970s and is still incredibly loved in my own home today. Classically made from the Northern regions of Italy and having just three simple ingredients, I have hijacked this recipe for my *cucina povera* kitchen and made it my own. The secret to this egg yolk cream is to use the freshest eggs you can find. I make zabaglione and spoon it immediately over seasonal soft fruit berries, pan fried peaches or poached pears. Served warm, zabaglione is very light on the palate and easy on your stomach too.

Preparation time: 4 minutes
Cooking time: 15 minutes
Serves: 4

5 egg yolks
4 tbsp marsala
2 tbsp granulated sugar
To serve:
20g dark chocolate (optional to grate)
20g amaretto biscuits, crushed

1. Place the egg yolks, sugar and marsala in a glass bowl and stir to combine fully. Place the bowl over a pan of simmering water. Make sure that the water does not touch the bottom of the bowl as it bubbles, as this may make the eggs scramble.
2. Use an electric whisk and whisk the mixture until the volume has almost doubled. This may take around 10–15 minutes, so be patient.
3. When the zabaglione is ready, spoon over your chosen fruit and sprinkle with crushed amaretto biscuits or grate a little dark chocolate over the top. Serve immediately.

Carmela's tip
Traditionally you would measure half an egg shell of marsala for each egg yolk used. You can freeze the egg whites to make a meringue at a later date.

Neapolitan Easter Tart

Pastiera napoletana

I am so pleased I don't have to wait until Easter for another slice of this moist and very delicate tart. It's a beautifully perfumed centrepiece, perfect for any celebration – not just Easter. Traditionally eaten and loved in Naples, in Campania, it is made with a buttery pastry base paired with rich ricotta, cooked grains and jewel-like orange peel. Grano cotto is available in Italian delicatessens and mixed through with the ricotta it adds a real substance and freshness to the tart.

Preparation time: 20 minutes
Pastry: 30 minutes chilling
Cooking time: 1 hour
Serves: 12

For the pastry:
350g '00' flour
200g butter, softened and cut into small cubes
100g caster sugar
1 tsp vanilla
2 large eggs
For the filling:
580g jar grano cotto
500g ricotta cheese
135g caster sugar
4 large egg yolks
2 tsp orangeflower water (or freshly squeezed orange)
100g orange peel, finely chopped
1 orange, zested
1 tsp icing sugar

1. Put the flour in a large bowl along with the butter. Use your fingertips to make breadcrumbs.
2. Sprinkle in the sugar and mix using a wooden spoon.

3. Pour in the vanilla and crack in the eggs. Stir and use a wooden spoon and your hands to form a dough. Wrap the dough in cling film and chill in the fridge for 30 minutes.

4. Preheat the oven to 180°C (gas 4).

5. Empty the grano cotto into a large bowl along with the fresh ricotta and mix. I like to use a fork for texture.

6. Sprinkle in the caster sugar and egg yolks, and mix with a metal spoon. Add the orangeflower water and chopped orange peel.

7. Add the orange zest and stir. Set the filling aside while you roll out the pastry.

8. Lightly dust your work surface with a little flour and roll out the pastry to 5mm thick. Use the pastry to line a 28cm tart tin with a loose bottom and trim off any excess around the edges.

9. Spoon the prepared filling into the tart case.

10. Take the trimmings of the pastry and roll strips of pastry around 2cm wide. Lay the strips in rows across the tart to create a lattice effect.

11. Bake for 1 hour until lightly golden and cooked through.

12. When cool, serve sliced and with a generous dusting of icing sugar alongside your favourite coffee.

Carmela's tip

Buy good quality ricotta from a delicatessen – most supermarket brands are very watery. Orangeflower water can be replaced with juice from a freshly squeezed orange.

Nutella and Hazelnut Cake

Torta cioccolata

I often find myself dipping a spoon into a jar of Nutella for a quick chocolate fix. The only problem is that when I start it is impossible to stop! This cake was always made by my mother as a mid-week treat. Sliced for our lunchboxes or heated through with a little gelato after dinner.

Preparation time: 15 minutes
Cooking time: 50–60 minutes
Serves: 8

175g butter
175g golden caster sugar
3 large eggs
200g self-raising flour
1 tsp baking powder
2 tsp cinnamon
4 tbsp milk
4 heaped tbsp Nutella
80g hazelnuts, halved

1. Grease and line a 20cm loose-bottomed tin.
2. Preheat the oven to 170°C (gas 4).
3. Place the butter, sugar, eggs, flour, baking powder, cinnamon and milk into a bowl and mix with a wooden spoon until fully combined.
4. Tip three quarters of the mixture into the cake tin and spread until level.
5. Spoon on the Nutella and level, then add the remaining cake mix and spread evenly.
6. The Nutella should be sandwiched between the cake batter.
7. Now sprinkle on the halved hazelnuts and push the odd one down with your fingertips.
8. Bake until cooked through.

Pear and Amaretto Pudding

Torta di pera e amaretto

I adore fresh fruit but have to say I am equally fond of tinned especially through the winter months. As a little girl I would love to sit by the fire with my dad as we shared a tin of peaches or pears as an after dinner pudding. Growing up, we would have tinned fruit at least twice a week – it is reasonably priced and means that you are able to create a quick pudding using store cupboard ingredients when the fruit bowl is empty.

Preparation time: 10 minutes
Cooking time: 1 hour
Serves: 6–8

2 x 400g tins pear halves in juice
60g amaretto biscuits crushed (use the hard biscuits)
200g caster sugar
200g butter
4 eggs
200g self-raising flour
1 tsp vanilla or the seeds from a pod
½ tsp ground cinnamon
2 tbsp milk
2 tbsp amaretto liqueur
250g mascarpone

1. Preheat the oven to 170°C (gas 4) and grease a 25cm round pie dish.
2. Drain the pears of all the juice and arrange them in the dish, cut side down. I recommend drinking the pear juice as it is just delicious!
3. Sprinkle the amaretto biscuits over the pears.
4. Put the butter and sugar in a large bowl and use a wooden spoon to cream them together. This will take around 4 minutes.
5. Slowly add the eggs one at a time and stir. Each time you crack in an egg, add 1 tbsp flour to prevent the batter from splitting.
6. Fold in the remaining flour along with the vanilla and cinnamon and stir well.
7. Pour in the milk, stir and spoon the mixture over the pears, then bake until golden.
8. Mix the amaretto liqueur through the mascarpone cheese with a wooden spoon, then serve alongside the pudding.

Orange Polenta Cake

Torta di polenta

Polenta is a dry grain also known as cornmeal and is ground from white or yellow maize. Loved by Italians, especially those in the Northern regions, some of my family in Torino and Verona use it daily: my father calls them 'polentone' as they eat so much. Depending on the region of Italy, polenta will be cooked in either milk or water and then heavily flavoured. It is a cheap and very simple ingredient to cook with – wonderful in both savoury and sweet dishes. Here is my delicious, moist and lightly perfumed orange polenta cake.

Preparation time: 15 minutes
Cooking time: 45–50 minutes
Serves: 8–10

For the cake:
250g butter
240g caster sugar
4 large eggs
130g instant polenta grain
200g self-raising flour (or plain flour and 2 tsp bicarbonate of soda)
Zest and juice of two oranges (reserve 100ml of juice for the glaze)
For the glaze:
100ml squeezed orange juice
100g golden caster sugar

1. Preheat the oven to 180°C (gas 4) and grease and line a 23cm loose-bottomed cake tin.
2. Cream the butter and sugar in a bowl until light and fluffy using an electric whisk or by hand with a wooden spoon.
3. Add the eggs one at a time and mix well.
4. Pour in the flour and polenta, and mix to incorporate.
5. Now add the zest from both oranges and the juice (reserving 100ml for the syrup).
6. Mix well and pour into the prepared cake tin. Level off the mixture and bake in the centre of the oven.

7. Test to ensure the cake is cooked. I use a long piece of spaghetti and prod the centre of the cake – the spaghetti should come out clean. Leave to cool on a wire rack.

8. For the syrup, mix the sugar and orange juice in a non-stick pan until the sugar has melted and simmer for about 5 minutes. It will thicken and become a syrup. Leave to cool.

9. When the cake and syrup are both cool, use a cocktail stick to prick holes in the cake and pour the syrup over, this allows some syrup to seep down into the centre of the cake.

10. Serve sliced, with a little mascarpone.

Panettone and Dark Chocolate Pudding

Budino con cioccolata

Panettone is a traditional Italian Christmas cake from the Milan area of Italy. A rich, egg-based bread studded with orange and lemon candied peel and voluptuous raisins, it is usually served torn and dipped into vin santo or sliced to eat alongside a cup of espresso. Every guest that enters my home through the month of December normally comes armed with a panettone. I will never complain as we love them and they are an essential part of our family Christmas. This is a great way to use up any leftovers if the cake becomes slightly stale.

Preparation time: 15 minutes
Cooking time: 35 minutes
Serves: 6–8

10g butter, for greasing
450g leftover panettone
70g dark chocolate chopped
2 tbsp ground amaretto biscuits
400ml semi-skimmed milk
100ml double cream
3 eggs
2 tbsp amaretto liqueur
30g light muscovado sugar
2 tbsp demerara sugar, to sprinkle
To serve:
2 tbsp amaretto liqueur
250g mascarpone

1. Preheat the oven to 170°C (gas 4) and grease a 23cm ovenproof dish with the butter.
2. Cut the panettone into large cubes and place in the prepared dish.
3. Tumble over the chopped dark chocolate. Make sure you tuck some of the chocolate under the panettone too.

4. Sprinkle over the ground amaretto biscuits.
5. Mix together the milk, double cream, eggs, amaretto liqueur and muscovado sugar in a large bowl. Whisk and gently pour over the panettonne bread. Try to soak every piece of panettone as you pour over the cream mixture and use your fingers to poke down any pieces of the panettone that are peeking up.
6. Sprinkle the demerara sugar over the top of the pudding.
7. Bake in the centre of the oven for 35 minutes until golden in colour.
8. Spoon the remaining amaretto liqueur into the mascarpone cheese and stir with a wooden spoon. Serve with the warm pudding.

Pistachio and Dark Chocolate Biscuits

Cantuccini con cioccolata e pistacchi

A traditional biscotti served with coffee in Italy. This biscuit has a firm bite and seems to take on any flavour it's given. I always have an array of nuts in my baking cupboard and, with this recipe, you can leave out the chocolate and just have the pistachio or maybe add the crunch of hazelnuts. Dried fruit would work equally very well.

Preparation time: 15 minutes
Cooking time: 24 minutes
Makes: 20 biscotti

250g strong white flour
150g caster sugar
1 tsp baking powder
100g dark chocolate, chopped
100g pistachios, chopped
1 tsp vanilla extract
1 clementine, zested
2 large eggs
Icing sugar to dust

1. Preheat the oven to 180°C (gas 4) and line two baking trays with parchment.
2. In a large bowl mix together the flour, sugar and baking powder.
3. Add the chopped chocolate, nuts, vanilla, zest and eggs.
4. Stir into a dough using a wooden spoon and then use your hands.
5. Sprinkle a little icing sugar over your work surface and roll the dough into a large wide sausage, then divide this into thirds. Icing sugar will not dry out the dough as flour would.
6. Slightly flatten the three dough portions, place them on a baking tray and bake for 20 minutes.

7. Remove from the oven and place onto a chopping board. Cut each sausage diagonally into biscotti-sized slices and place each one back onto the baking tray. Pop back into the oven for 2–3 minutes.

8. Serve with vin santo or coffee.

Carmela's tip

Store biscotti in an airtight container and they will easily keep for a week.

Rice Cake with Ricotta and Lemon

Torta con riso, ricotta e limone

I always try to have just a small slice of this torta, but find within minutes I am slicing myself another generous piece. Usually made by Nonna at Easter for the whole family, it is a traditional feast tart from the south of Italy. With moist ricotta, soft pudding rice, zesty lemon and fabulous aromatic strega, this torta really comes alive. You can substitute the strega with another spirit, such as rum or amaretto if preferred.

Preparation and chilling time: 40 minutes
Cooking time: 1 hour 30 minutes
Serves: 8

For the pastry:
300g '00' flour
Pinch of salt
85g granulated sugar
1 egg white (reserve the yolk for glazing)
2 tsp vanilla extract
85ml extra virgin olive oil
½ lemon, juiced
For the filling:
250g pudding rice
100g granulated sugar
3 eggs
550g fresh ricotta
2 tsp vanilla extract
1 lemon, zest and juice
30ml strega liqueur
25g butter

1. In a bowl, mix together the flour, salt and sugar. Make a well in the centre and add the egg white, vanilla, olive oil and lemon juice. Use a wooden spoon to combine the mixture to form a dough.

2. Lightly flour the work surface and tip out the dough. Knead the dough for 5 minutes until it is smooth.

3. Wrap the dough in cling film and chill in the fridge for 20 minutes.

4. Roll out the chilled dough to the thickness of a pound coin and use it to line a 22cm loose-bottomed tart case. Trim off the excess pastry using a knife and set to one side, wrapped in cling film, to make the lattice top.

5. Place the tart case back into the fridge to chill whilst you make the filling.

6. Preheat the oven to 180°C (gas 4) and put a baking tray into the oven.

7. Cook the pudding rice according to the packet instructions until just tender. Drain and set aside.

8. In a mixing bowl, combine the sugar and eggs, using a wooden spoon. Crumble in the ricotta and mix.

9. Add the cooked pudding rice, vanilla, lemon zest, juice, strega and butter.

10. Mix well for a minute to combine fully all of the ingredients, then spoon the mixture into the chilled pastry case.

11. Roll out the remaining pastry dough to the thickness of a 50p coin and slice the dough into long strips. Lay the strips in a lattice effect over the tart.

12. Whisk the egg yolk and, using a pastry brush, egg wash the lattice pastry.

13. Gently place the tart onto the baking tray and bake for 1 hour 30mins.

14. Serve sliced, with coffee.

Ricotta Cheesecake

Torta di ricotta

A moist ricotta cake showcasing one of my favourite Italian liqueurs. Strega is amber and bold in colour and has a combination of saffron, mint, fennel and a further 50 spices and herbs. Used in cakes and biscuits, strega adds warmth to any Italian homemade bake.

Preparation time: 15 minutes
Cooking time: 1 hour 10 minutes
Serves: 12

1200g ricotta
200g granulated sugar
4 large eggs, separated
1 large lemon, zest only
1 tsp vanilla extract
2 tbsp strega
1 orange, zested

1. Preheat the oven to 180°C (gas 4).
2. Beat together the ricotta, sugar, egg yolks, lemon zest, vanilla and strega for around 3 minutes. It's easiest to do this with an electric stand mixer, but a wooden spoon and large bowl will also be fine.
3. In a separate bowl, beat the egg whites for two minutes until you reach soft peaks.
4. Fold the egg whites through the ricotta mixture.
5. Pour the mixture into a 22cm spring form cake tin and bake for 1 hour 30 minutes.
6. Allow the cake to cool in the oven with the door ajar.
7. Remove from the oven and allow the cake to cool completely, cover with cling film and refrigerate for 3 hours.
8. Serve sliced with a little grated orange zest.

Panna cotta

Panna cotta

I feel like I'm always saying, "This is my favourite pudding," but I think panna cotta truly is. Panna cotta, meaning cooked cream, is a wonderful summer pudding – light, fresh and simple, with a smooth silky texture, and it is easier to make than you may think.

Preparation time: 10 minutes
Cooking time: 4 minutes
Setting time: 3 hours
Serves: 4

250ml semi-skimmed milk
250ml double cream
1 vanilla pod, seeds and pod
25g caster sugar
3 gelatine leaves
20g dark chocolate, grated
350g seasonal berries

1. Place the gelatine leaves in a bowl of cold water and soak them for 5 minutes.
2. Combine the milk, cream, and the seeds and casing from the vanilla pod in a small saucepan. Sprinkle in the sugar.
3. Bring the mixture to a light simmer and remove from the heat. Allow the sugar to dissolve.
4. Remove the vanilla pod casing and discard.
5. Squeeze the gelatine leaves to remove excess water and place them into the hot milky mixture. Stir until they have dissolved.
6. Pour the mixture into wine glasses or ramekins, place on a tray and pop in the fridge for at least 3 hours to chill and set.
7. Serve the panna cotta with grated dark chocolate and a selection of seasonal berries.

Tiramisu

Tiramisu

One of the most famous and well-loved Italian desserts there is, this pudding truly lives up to its name 'tiramisu' meaning pull me up! Although said to have been invented in Siena, tiramisu is made throughout Italy. Make tiramisu ahead of time and allow it to set in the fridge for at least 4 hours. You can add seasonal fresh fruit to the top or just grate some dark chocolate over the top.

Preparation time: 20 minutes
Setting time: 4–6 hours
Serves: 6–8

300ml strong black coffee
6 tbsp amaretto liqueur
6 large eggs
6 tbsp granulated sugar
500g mascarpone
750g savoiardi biscuits (known as ladies' fingers)
100g amaretto biscuits, crushed
20g dark chocolate

1. Make the strong coffee and allow it to cool. Add the amaretto and set to one side.
2. Separate the eggs. Whites in one bowl and yolks in another. Add the sugar to the egg yolks and whisk for 5 minutes, until creamy.
3. Add the mascarpone cheese to the egg yolk mixture and combine. Stir with a wooden spoon and then whisk for 1 minute to remove any lumps.
4. Wash the whisk, then whisk the egg whites until stiff peaks are formed.
5. Gently fold in the egg whites to the mascarpone mixture, half the mixture at a time.
6. Take your trifle dish or individual glasses and start layering up the ingredients.
7. Quickly dip each biscuit into the coffee liqueur mixture and place in your dish.

8. Complete one biscuit layer then spoon on a layer of the cream mixture and level. Sprinkle over a little of the crushed amaretto biscuits. Then return to dipping and layering the biscuits, add the cream and amaretto biscuits.
9. Continue until you have three sets of layers, finishing with the cream on top.
10. Chill in the fridge for at least 4–6 hours. If you use glasses or ramekins they will only need 2 hours to chill.
11. Serve with grated dark chocolate and a sprinkling of crushed amaretto biscuits.

Carmela's tip

Try using panettone or pandoro instead of the savoiardi biscuits (only as a base layer). This will add a change of texture and will produce pudding resembling a trifle.

Zabaglione Ice Cream
Zabaglione gelato

An authentic gelateria in Italy is an essential place to visit; I look out for them and then generally beat the children to the queue, as it is – with no doubt whatsoever – the best ice cream in the world. There is nothing better than seeing small children with their faces pushed up against the glass fridge deciding what flavour to choose. For me, hazelnut wins every time, but this zabaglione gelato is simple and versatile, and can easily be flavoured using berries, nuts and even chopped torrone.

Preparation time: 20 minutes
Cooking time: 10 minutes
Freezing time: 2 hours
Serves: 6

4 large egg yolks
120g caster sugar
140ml marsala
150ml whipping cream
100g chopped strawberries (optional)

1. Place the egg yolks and sugar into a large, heatproof bowl. Whisk until pale and light.
2. Pour the marsala into the egg yolks and whisk some more to combine.
3. Place a saucepan on the hob with some simmering water in the base. then place your mixing bowl over the pan, making sure that the bowl does not touch the water.
4. Whisk the egg yolks with an electric whisk until their volume has almost doubled. This may take up to 10 minutes.
5. Remove the bowl from the heat and dip the base into cold water to cool it fully and stop the mixture from cooking any more.
6. Whip the cream until it holds its shape, then add it to the cold egg mixture and combine. Add the chopped strawberries, if using.
7. Pour the mixture into a container and place in the freezer for at least 2 hours. Alternatively churn in an ice cream maker for around 45 minutes and freeze.
8. Transfer to the fridge about 30 minutes before serving.
9. Serve either in a cornet or chilled bowl.

Italian Store Cupboard Essentials

There are a few ingredients that I need in order to feel complete whilst cooking in my kitchen. Now, to say that it is just a few may be a little white lie, because as I am writing I find myself adding ingredient upon ingredient to my list. However, garlic, olive oil, anchovies, pancetta and dried pasta are the essentials I would have to start with and could certainly never be without. A well-stocked store cupboard will save you money in the long run, and if you have a little of everything you can muster up any number of delicious meals at the drop of a hat when faced with unexpected company or in need of a quick and easy fuel-stop.

Essential Ingredients

In order to produce simple, affordable, healthy dishes you will need to have a well-stocked larder and fridge. Here are my essential ingredients and staples to help you in your cooking. Alongside all of these, you will just need to buy fresh meat, fish and seafood.

Oils:
Olive oil: To drizzle and to lightly fry
Rapeseed oil: To shallow fry
Extra virgin olive oil: For finishing off dishes and salads

Vinegars:
A must in any salad dressing. My favourite is always the deep, dark colour of the balsamic from Modena.
Balsamic: from Modena
Red wine vinegar
White wine vinegar

Tins:
A store cupboard full of tinned tomatoes and beans provides the basis to lots of simple *cucina povera* style dishes.
Tinned tomatoes: chopped and plum
Beans: cannellini, chick peas, butter beans, borlotti beans
Passata: my favourite is *Cirio Rustica*
Tomato purée: to add flavour to soups, stocks and sauces
Olives: variety of green and black with stones, in brine
Capers: in brine. These berries add texture to dishes

Anchovies: in brine. These subtly melt away whilst leaving a pleasant depth of saltiness to any dish

Dried Herbs:
An essential store cupboard ingredient. Just always remember that dried herbs have a more concentrated flavour and should be used sparingly.
Fennel seeds
Chilli flakes
Oregano
Basil
Marjoram
Thyme
Stock cubes: chicken and vegetable

Fresh Herbs:
It is always preferable to use fresh herbs wherever possible as they add a delicate flavour to any given dish.
Rosemary
Basil
Oregano
Sage
Marjoram
Thyme
Chilli
Parsley
Bay leaves

Flour:
'00' flour: an essential flour for pasta making, bread, cakes and pizzas
Plain flour: a universal ingredient
Self-raising flour: a staple flour for cake making
Strong white bread flour: I use combined with other flours to change consistency of dough
Semolina flour: perfect for bread and pasta

Baking:
Hard amaretto biscuits: I crush them and use them as a topping for tiramisu, cakes or ice cream
Vanilla: extract and fresh pods
Pane di angeli: a traditional powder used in a range of Italian cakes and desserts

Dried pasta and grains:
Spaghetti, bucatini, ditalini, penne, trofie, rigatoni, pastina
Polenta: instant grain
Lentils: red and green
Rice: arborio, carnaroli and vialone nano

Sugar:
Caster
Granulated
Golden
Demarera

Dairy:
Cream: single and double
Milk: I use semi-skimmed
Butter: unsalted is preferable
Eggs: all of the eggs used in this book are large

Cheese:
Ricotta: ricotta does not melt and means re-cooked. Bought from a deli only, supermarket ricotta is too wet.
Mozzarella: made with cow's milk. Ideal to freeze and have in stock for layered pasta and pizza.
Buffalo mozzarella: torn into a salad, never cooked as it is delicious simply dressed with a little extra virgin olive oil and balsamic.
Parmesan: grated into pasta, risotto and more (never buy ready grated Parmesan).
Pecorino: sheep's cheese. An alternative to Parmesan.
Provolone: Southern Italian cheese, smooth in texture. Sliced finely and eaten with bread, my father Rocco's favourite.
Gorgonzola: mild and creamy with a blue vein.
Taleggio: made with cow's milk and is semi-soft. Very delicious.
Mascarpone: perfect for my tiramisu, in desserts and stirred through roasted butternut squash and filled into ravioli.
Fontina: semi-hard cheese, creamy in texture and perfect for melting.

Cured meat:
Prosciutto crudo: Parma ham
Prosciutto cotto: cooked ham
Pancetta: from the pork belly area, finely sliced or cubed
Guanciale: pigs' cheeks, delicious

finely cubed in place of pancetta in a carbonara

Salami: milano, napoli, ventricine, finnochiona

Mortadella: re-formed pork, very delicious finely sliced as part of an antipasti platter

Bresaola: air-dried lean beef

Coppa: dry-cured whole pork shoulder or neck, sliced finely

Fresh Vegetables:

Fresh vine tomatoes: cherry, plum

Garlic: fresh bulbs

Onions, celery and carrots to make the perfect soffritto

Liqueur:

Amaretto

Tia Maria

Frangelico

Marsala

White Vermouth: an alternative for wine in risotto

Chambord

Index

amaretto biscuits
    Auntie Anna's Amaretto and Dark Chocolate
      Cake 185
    Panettone and Dark Chocolate Pudding 198–9
    Pear and Amaretto Pudding 195
    Tiramisu 206–7
anchovies
    Bucatini with Anchovies and Capers 141
    Eggs Filled with Tuna 4
    Filled Courgette Flowers 116–17
    Filled Mussels 98–9
    Green Anchovies 6
    Green Sauce 30
    Pizza Puttanesca 62–3
    Spaghetti with Broccoli and Toasted
      Breadcrumbs 164–5
Artichokes, Stuffed 14–15
Asparagus Pesto, Seasonal 37
aubergines
    Aubergine Dip 12
    Aubergine Parcels 2
    Softened Sicilian Aubergines 13
    Solidea's Parmigiana 130–1
    Stuffed Aubergines 134–5

beef
    Beef Steak in Tomato Sauce 68
    Bolognese Sauce 26–7
    Meatballs 80
    Sunday Lasagne 168–9
    Zia Maria's Italian Meatloaf 87–8
bread
    Bread Balls 57
    Bread Salad 110
    Bread Soup with Cannellini Beans 25
    Bruschetta 3
    Fennel Seed Bread 46–7
    Flat Topped Bread 50–1
    Mediterranean Filled Loaf 52–3
    Mozzarella Sandwich 122
    Olive Bread 54–5
    Parmesan Breadsticks 56
    Semolina Bread 66
    Twisted Bread Sticks with Olive, Parmesan and
      Oregano 64–5
broad beans: Pancetta, Broad Bean and Pea
    Risotto 174–5

broccoli: Spaghetti with Broccoli and Toasted
    Breadcrumbs 164–5

calamari
    Baby Octopus Salad 90–1
    Filled Calamari in a Tomato Sauce 96–7
    Linguine with Squid 144
cannellini beans
    Bread Soup with Cannellini Beans 25
    Italian Sausage with Cannellini Beans and
      Polenta 172–3
    Pasta with Cannellini Beans 153
    Simple Beans 126
Cannelloni 142–3
capers
    Baked Sea Bream Parcel 93
    Bucatini with Anchovies and Capers 141
    Eggs Filled with Tuna 4
    Filled Mussels 98–9
    Filled Romano Peppers 114–15
    Green Sauce 30
    Pizza Puttanesca 62–3
    Tomatoes Filled with Tuna 19
chicken
    Breaded Chicken Cutlets 70–1
    Chicken Stock 28
    Hunter's Chicken 69
chickpeas
    Macaroni with Chickpeas 146
    Simple Beans 126
chocolate
    Auntie Anna's Amaretto and Dark Chocolate
      Cake 185
    Nutella and Hazelnut Cake 194
    Panettone and Dark Chocolate Pudding 198–9
    Pistachio and Dark Chocolate Biscuits 200–1
coffee
    Coffee Granita 184
    Tiramisu 206–7
courgettes
    Courgette Fritters 133
    Filled Courgette Flowers 116–17
    Frittata with Courgette and Potato 118
    Marrow Parmigiana with Italian Sausage Sauce
      120–1
    Pan Fried Courgettes 9
cucina povera vii–viii

dandelion leaves
  Lamb and Escarole Bake 78–9
  Spring Dandelion Greens with Chilli and
    Garlic 132

eel
  Eel in a Tomato Sauce 94
  Roast Eel with Breadcrumbs 95
eggs
  Eggs Filled with Tuna 4
  Frittata with Courgette and Potato 118
  Lamb and Escarole Bake 78–9
  Lamb, Pea and Egg Bake 75
  Marsala and Egg Yolk Froth 191
  Parmesan Soufflé 10
  Pizza Florentina 60
  Simple Egg Pasta Dough 138–9
  Tiny Pasta with Egg 170

Fava Beans and Pecorino on Toasted Bread 5
fennel
  Bruschetta 3
  Fennel and Parmesan Salad 111
fennel seeds
  Fennel Biscuits 186–7
  Fennel Seed Bread 46–7
figs: Nonna's Figs with Gorgonzola and Parma
  Ham 8
fish and seafood
  Baby Octopus Salad 90–1
  Baked Red Mullet 92
  Baked Sea Bream Parcel 93
  Fish Baked in Salt 100–1
  Fish Stock 29
  Fried Seafood 102–3
  Linguine with Clams 104–5
  Salt Cod with Tomatoes and Potatoes 108
  see also anchovies; calamari; eel; mussels; red
    mullet; sea bass; tuna
Fritto Misto 102–3

Gnocchi 158–9
  Spinach and Ricotta Gnocchi 166–7
gorgonzola
  Gorgonzola Sauce 42
  Nonna's Figs with Gorgonzola and Parma Ham 8
Green Bean Salad 119
Gremolata 41

ice cream
  Limoncello Ice Cream 190
  Summer Fruit Ice Cream 189
  Zabaglione Ice Cream 208
lamb
  Lamb and Escarole Bake 78–9

Lamb, Pea and Egg Bake 75
lemons
  Ciambella Cake 182–3
  Lemon and Polenta Cake 188
  Limoncello Ice Cream 190
  Rice Cake with Ricotta and Lemon 202–3
  Zesty Sauce 41
lentils
  Filled Romano Peppers with lentils 124
  Lentil and White Onion Soup 31
liver
  Fried Offal and Pork 82
  Liver and Onions 76–7

Minestrone 32–3
mozzarella
  Baked Rigatoni 140
  Cannelloni 142–3
  Filled Calzone Pizza 48–9
  Filled Romano Peppers 114–15
  Filled Romano Peppers with lentils 124
  Marrow Parmigiana with Italian Sausage Sauce
    120–1
  Mediterranean Filled Loaf 52–3
  Mozzarella Sandwich 122
  Pasta from Beautiful Sorrento 147
  Pasta Shells Filled with Ricotta and Mozzarella
    150–1
  Pizza Florentina 60
  Polenta Pizza 180
  Risotto Balls 11
  Solidea's Parmigiana 130–1
  Stuffed Portobello Mushrooms 16–17
  Sunday Lasagne 168–9
  Tomato and Mozzarella Salad 18
mushrooms
  Cannelloni 142–3
  Filled Calzone Pizza 48–9
  Mushrooms with Thyme 7
  Risotto with Mushrooms 176–7
  Stuffed Aubergines 134–5
  Stuffed Portobello Mushrooms 16–17
mussels
  Filled Mussels 98–9
  Mussels with Tomatoes 106–7

olives
  Baked Red Mullet 92
  Bucatini with Anchovies and Capers 141
  Filled Romano Peppers 114–15
  Hunter's Chicken 69
  Olive Bread 54–5
  Pesto with Basil and Olives 22–3
  Rabbit with Tomatoes and Olives 86
  Salt Cod with Tomatoes and Potatoes 108

Twisted Bread Sticks with Olive, Parmesan and Oregano 64–5
oranges
Neapolitan Easter Tart 192–3
Orange Polenta Cake 196–7

pancetta
Macaroni with Chickpeas 146
Pancetta, Broad Bean and Pea Risotto 174–5
Pasta Shells with Butter and Pancetta 152
Pasta with Cannellini Beans 153
Roasted Pheasant with Pancetta and White Wine 81
Spaghetti Carbonara 162
Stuffed Aubergines 134–5
Panna Cotta 205
Panzanella 110
Parma ham
Nonna's Figs with Gorgonzola and Parma Ham 8
Zia Maria's Italian Meatloaf 87–8
Parmesan
Fennel and Parmesan Salad 111
Parmesan Breadsticks 56
Parmesan Soufflé 10
Spaghetti Carbonara 162
Spinach and Ricotta Gnocchi 166–7
Spinach Pesto 136
Stuffed Artichokes 14–15
Twisted Bread Sticks with Olive, Parmesan and Oregano 64–5
pasta
Baked Rigatoni 140
Bucatini with Anchovies and Capers 141
Cannelloni 142–3
Ditalini with Peas 145
Linguine with Squid 144
Macaroni with Chickpeas 146
Orecchiette Pasta with Turnip Tops 148–9
Pasta from Beautiful Sorrento 147
Pasta Shells Filled with Ricotta and Mozzarella 150–1
Pasta Shells with Butter and Pancetta 152
Pasta with Cannellini Beans 153
Pasta with Potatoes 154–5
Penne with Chilli and Garlic 156
Rocco's Spaghetti with Garlic and Oil 157
Simple Egg Pasta Dough 138–9
Spaghetti Carbonara 162
Spaghetti with Baby Plum Tomatoes 163
Spaghetti with Broccoli and Toasted Breadcrumbs 164–5
Spinach and Ricotta Ravioli 160–1
Sunday Lasagne 168–9
Tagliatelle Bolognese 27
Tiny Pasta with Egg 170

Pear and Amaretto Pudding 195
peas
Ditalini with Peas 145
Lamb, Pea and Egg Bake 75
Pancetta, Broad Bean and Pea Risotto 174–5
Risotto with Peas 178–9
peppers
Aubergine Dip 12
Bruschetta 3
Filled Baby Peppers 112–13
Filled Calzone Pizza 48–9
Filled Romano Peppers 114–15
Filled Romano Peppers with lentils 124
Fried Offal and Pork 82
Hunter's Chicken 69
Mediterranean Filled Loaf 52–3
Roasted Tomato and Pepper Soup 36
Slow Stewed Peppers 129
pesto
Bruschetta 3
Pesto with Basil and Olives 22–3
Seasonal Asparagus Pesto 37
Spinach Pesto 136
Stuffed Portobello Mushrooms 16–17
Sundried Tomato Pesto 39
pheasant: Roasted Pheasant with Pancetta and White Wine 81
pizza
Filled Calzone Pizza 48–9
Nonna Carmela's Pizza Doughballs 44–5
Pizza Dough Perfection 58–9
Pizza Florentina 60
Pizza Marinara 61
Pizza Puttanesca 62–3
Pizza Topping Sauce 35
Polenta Pizza 180
polenta
Italian Sausage with Cannellini Beans and Polenta 172–3
Lemon and Polenta Cake 188
Orange Polenta Cake 196–7
Polenta Pizza 180
Potato Dumplings 158–9
pork
Bolognese Sauce 26–7
Fried Offal and Pork 82
Meat Sauce 34
Meatballs 80
Pasta Shells Filled with Ricotta and Mozzarella 150–1
Pork Stew 84–5
Rolled Pork Escalope 83
Sunday Lasagne 168–9
Zia Maria's Italian Meatloaf, beef 87–8
potatoes

Frittata with Courgette and Potato 118
Italian Roasted Potatoes with Garlic and
  Rosemary 128
Pasta with Potatoes 154–5
Potato Dumplings 158–9
Salt Cod with Tomatoes and Potatoes 108
Simple Potato Salad 127

rabbit
  Braised Rabbit with White Wine and Fresh
    Herbs 72–3
  Rabbit with Tomatoes and Olives 86
rice
  Rice Cake with Ricotta and Lemon 202–3
  Rice Salad 123
  see also risotto
ricotta
  Aubergine Parcels 2
  Cannelloni 142–3
  Filled Courgette Flowers 116–17
  Homemade Ricotta 20
  Neapolitan Easter Tart 192–3
  Pasta Shells Filled with Ricotta and Mozzarella
    150–1
  Rice Cake with Ricotta and Lemon 202–3
  Ricotta Cheesecake 204
  Spinach and Ricotta Gnocchi 166–7
  Spinach and Ricotta Ravioli 160–1
risotto
  Pancetta, Broad Bean and Pea Risotto 174–5
  Risotto Balls 11
  Risotto with Mushrooms 176–7
  Risotto with Peas 178–9

Salsa Verde 30
sausages
  Italian Sausage with Cannellini Beans and
    Polenta 172–3
  Marrow Parmigiana with Italian Sausage
    Sauce 120–1
Spaghetti Aglio e Olio 157
spinach
  Pizza Florentina 60
  Seasonal Spinach with Crushed Tomatoes 125
  Spinach and Ricotta Gnocchi 166–7
  Spinach and Ricotta Ravioli 160–1
  Spinach Pesto 136
storecupboard essentials 209–12
Stromboli 52–3

Tiramisu 206–7
tomatoes
  Baked Sea Bream Parcel 93
  Beef Steak in Tomato Sauce 68
  Bolognese Sauce 26–7

Braised Rabbit with White Wine and Fresh
  Herbs 72–3
Bread Salad 110
Bread Soup with Cannellini Beans 25
Breaded Veal with Tomato Salad 74
Bruschetta 3
Bucatini with Anchovies and Capers 141
Cannelloni 142–3
Eel in a Tomato Sauce 94
Filled Calamari in a Tomato Sauce 96–7
Filled Romano Peppers 114–15
Flat Topped Bread 50–1
Hunter's Chicken 69
Italian Sausage with Cannellini Beans and
  Polenta 172–3
Linguine with Clams 104–5
Marrow Parmigiana with Italian Sausage
  Sauce 120–1
Meat Sauce 34
Minestrone 32–3
Mussels with Tomatoes 106–7
Pasta from Beautiful Sorrento 147
Pasta with Potatoes 154–5
Penne with Chilli and Garlic 156
Pizza Topping Sauce 35
Pork Stew 84–5
Rabbit with Tomatoes and Olives 86
Rice Salad 123
Roasted Tomato and Pepper Soup 36
Salt Cod with Tomatoes and Potatoes 108
Seasonal Spinach with Crushed Tomatoes 125
Simple Tomato Sauce 38
Slow Stewed Peppers 129
Solidea's Parmigiana 130–1
Spaghetti with Baby Plum Tomatoes 163
Stuffed Aubergines 134–5
Sunday Lasagne 168–9
Sundried Tomato Pesto 39
Tomato and Mozzarella Salad 18
Tomatoes Filled with Tuna 19
tuna
  Eggs Filled with Tuna 4
  Tomatoes Filled with Tuna 19
turnips: Orecchiette Pasta with Turnip Tops
  148–9

veal: Breaded Veal with Tomato Salad 74
Vegetable Stock 40

White Sauce 24

Zabaglione 191
  Zabaglione Ice Cream 208